Read It Aloud!

Using Literature in the Secondary Content Classroom

Judy S. Richardson
Virginia Commonwealth University
Richmond, Virginia, USA

INTERNATIONAL
**Reading
Association**

800 Barksdale Road, PO Box 8139
Newark, Delaware 19714-8139, USA
www.reading.org

KH

Director of Publications   Joan M. Irwin
Assistant Director of Publications   Jeanette K. Moss
Editor in Chief, Books   Matthew W. Baker
Permissions Editor   Janet S. Parrack
Associate Editor   Tori Mello
Assistant Editor   Sarah Rutigliano
Acquisitions and Communications Coordinator   Amy T. Roff
Publications Coordinator   Beth Doughty
Association Editor   David K. Roberts
Production Department Manager   Iona Sauscermen
Art Director   Boni Nash
Electronic Publishing Supervisor   Wendy A. Mazur
Electronic Publishing Specialist   Anette Schütz-Ruff
Electronic Publishing Specialist   Cheryl J. Strum
Electronic Publishing Assistant   Peggy Mason

Project Editor   Janet S. Parrack

Photo Credits   Cover, Arni Katz/The Stock Solution

Library of Congress Cataloging in Publication Data
   Richardson, Judy S., 1945–
   Read it aloud! using literature in the secondary content classroom / Judy S. Richardson.
      p.   cm.
   Includes bibliographical references and index.
   ISBN 0-87207-256-8 (alk paper)
   1. Oral reading.   2. Reading (Secondary)   3.Content area reading.   I. Title: Read it aloud!   II. Title.
LB1573.5.R53   2000
428'.4'0712—dc21   99-049355

Fourth Printing, February 2004   Printed in Canada

12/21/04

To middle and high school teachers
who are always seeking effective ways
to engage their students.

Contents

Preface

love to read, and I want all of my students to love to read also. Sadly, many do not. However, enthusiasm is contagious. I noticed even in my early teaching days that my students would become calmer and more attentive when I read aloud to them, even pieces from a "deadly dull" textbook.

One day I brought in a book to read—to myself—during my lunch break and I set it on my desk. My students noticed the book. They commented on its thickness and its cover and they wondered what it was about: "Gosh, Mrs. Richardson, are you going to read that whole book?" "Is it good?" "Do you really like to read?" Their questions were tinged with curiosity. I asked what they were reading, and they replied, "Nothing." They said that they used to read—in elementary school—but not anymore. They had loved when teachers read to them and had wanted to finish what the teacher had started. But now? No one read to them anymore, neither parents nor teachers, so I took a few minutes and read a passage from my book to each of my classes that day. Their reactions changed my perspective. Why do we think that middle and high school students are "too big" for read-alouds? My 12th graders loved the experience. Ever since, I have been on the lookout for great read-alouds to share with students.

My purpose in writing this book is simple: to spread the joy of reading. Constructing lessons that are interesting and relevant should be every teacher's goal. I will demonstrate how seamlessly teachers can add literature to a lesson, why they should, and that the rewards can be immense. The activities require very little instructional time. By showing how read-alouds and read-alongs can be used in content classrooms, teachers and students will see the array of resources, which will enrich learning while giving pleasure. When students see their teachers reading, they begin to understand how extensive reading engages and teaches us, and they become more likely to try it themselves.

The following story illustrates how contagious a read-aloud can be. A few years ago, our family was moving and had to spend a very long week in a motel room. My then 14-year-old son and I stopped by our old house to pick up the mail. In the mail was the *Journal of Reading*, which contained my column, "A read-aloud for music classrooms." My son saw my column and asked me to tell him about this read-aloud. This is the same child who previously had asked me not to recommend any books to him because his tastes were not the same as mine and he would be unlikely to enjoy anything I recommended. I read him the selection from *After Long Silence* by Sheri Tepper (described in Chapter 6 of this volume). He asked me so many questions about the excerpt that I finally had to tell him he was asking for the book itself. He demanded that we go to the library to request the book. I was thrilled when my son read and enjoyed the book.

In this book I include excerpts from many literature genres—children's literature, young adult literature, contemporary adult fiction, mysteries, classics, biographies, information books, and documentaries. The selections are based on the "Read-It-Aloud" columns published from 1994 to 1998 in the *Journal of Reading* and the *Journal of Adolescent & Adult Literacy*. A brief introduction to each selection provides background. Sometimes I describe how I discovered the book, which demonstrates the many ways readers may encounter books and make reading choices. Often, encounters are unplanned and personal—adults seldom read from assigned lists. When I tell secondary students how I discovered a book, they are often intrigued and become more willing to read voluntarily, because they see that reading is not so much a "have to" chore as it is a "want to" experience.

The introductions are followed by brief descriptions of the selections. An excerpt is provided and, finally, several activities for instruction in the content area and language arts are given. In addition to the selections included in this book, I encourage teachers to read the entire resource not only for their own enjoyment, but also because they may find other portions to read aloud.

The selections are grouped by content. Each chapter features a content area for easy access by busy teachers who want to find selections specific to their daily instruction. Each chapter begins with a brief introduction of the content area and its focus. Next, three or four read-aloud read-along selections are presented in detail. Following the lengthier selections are some abbreviated selections.

Appendix A lists other read-alouds and read-alongs that I and other teachers have discovered, but were not used in this book. I hope that teachers will read all the read-aloud selections because many can be applied to other content areas. Teachers will see possibilities I have overlooked. When you read *Read It Aloud!*, you will see why the selections included here can engage your students, as they have mine. You will discover, collect, and share your own great read-alouds and read-alongs.

Acknowledgments

I am grateful to the following colleagues who advised about the content area information for the selections in this book:

Dr. Richard Rezba
Dr. Leila Christenbury
Dr. Ena Gross
Dr. John Rossi
Dr. Daisy Reed
Dr. Sandra Guerard

I also thank my coauthors of the column "Read It Aloud" in the *Journal of Adolescent & Adult Literacy*:

Margaret Breen, coauthor of "A nonfiction resource to whet appetites"
Nancy S. Smith, coauthor of "Launching into space"
R. Jeffrey Cantrell, coauthor of "What is poetry?"
Dennis B. Wimer and Julie Counts, coauthors of "A read-aloud for romantics and realists"
Jane Brady Matanzo, first author of "An operatic read-aloud for music and art"
Lee Carleton, coauthor of "A read-aloud for students of English as a second language"
Mary Seward, coauthor of "Of libraries and adult beginning readers"
Joseph Boyle, coauthor of "A read aloud for discussing disabilities"
Mark A. Forget, coauthor of "A read-aloud for algebra and geometry classes"

Why Read Aloud?

One person reads aloud to another. Parents read aloud to their small children. Sometimes teachers read aloud to their classes. The content and context shift, but the practice has been a favorite for as long as there have been readers. When A. Sterl Artley (1975) asked teachers what they remembered about their former teachers, read-alouds were reported as a big favorite. Patricia Martin (1993) wrote that reading aloud is "rooted in history" (p. 16); the activity was enjoyed by pioneer families and used to entertain workers in factories. Martin's "Rules for the Road" provided tips for read-aloud partners. Peggy Daisy (1993) listed read-alouds as one of three ways to promote literacy at any age. Reading aloud to other class members provided her preservice teachers with "a reading strategy to promote an intergenerational continuity of lifelong reading to others" (p. 437). Ninth graders who read aloud their own writing to other students realized "the power of the spoken word and of the bond that develops between speaker/oral reader and audience" (Megyeri, 1993, p. 189). For middle school students, read-alouds provide opportunities to enjoy the classics and Newbery Medal and Honor Award books (Norton, 1992).

Advocates of read-alouds include Jim Trelease (1989), who wrote *The New Read-Aloud Handbook*, his version of a read-aloud program that parents can implement, and *Hey! Listen to This: Stories to Read Aloud* (1992), which provides further read-aloud suggestions, including many for teenagers. Regie Routman (1991) suggested that "reading aloud should take place daily at all grade levels, including junior high and high school" (p. 32). When Janice Gallagher (1987) described the reading bonds her family formed, reading aloud to share literature with her spouse and adolescent children was an important aspect of her "read with your eyes; listen with your heart" commentary.

One of the greatest authors of the 20th century, Jean Paul Sartre (1964), related in his autobiography *Words* that he could not make a connection to books and reading until he asked his mother to read aloud to him. His grandfather had given him *The Tales of Maurice Bouchor*, but Sartre could not unlock the story:

> On the verge of tears, I finally put them on my mother's lap. She raised her eyes from her sewing: "What would you like me to read to you, darling?" I took pleasure in her unfinished sentences, in her faltering words, in her sudden assurance, which quickly weakened and fled, petering out melodiously, and which, after a silence, came together again. (p. 45)

What Research and Theory Indicate About Reading Aloud

The now classic study *How in the World Do Students Read?* (Elley, 1992) compared the reading scores of 9- to 14-year-olds in 32 systems of education. Although the United States produced "relatively high scores at the 9-year-old level" (p. xi), [they] were lower than several countries at the 14-year-old level. One major finding of the study was that "frequent story reading aloud by teach-

ers" (p. xii) was a factor consistently differentiating high-scoring countries.

In a recent study conducted through the National Reading Research Center, Baumann and Duffy (1997) discussed the topic *Engaged Reading for Pleasure and Learning*. Some key ideas reported for the middle and high school student include using multiple documents for learning and discussing books. A key idea reported for teachers is their engagement in research by reading and researching widely. Read-alouds are a sound way to promote wide reading in many resources.

In a study of 44 resistant secondary readers, Bintz (1993) discovered that positive role models influenced the performance of high school students. He points out that "out-of-school reading activities have a strong association with reading achievement" (p. 614). Logically, when teachers share their own out-of-school reading via read-alouds, students will surely grasp the relationship of reading to content and to real life. Research by Duchein and Mealey (1993) indicated that more than two thirds of their subjects were read to prior to starting school, and more than one half were read to by primary teachers, but the practice had ceased for most by third grade. However, the researchers also found that "those teachers who did read aloud during grades four to six and into middle and high school grades made significant, positive, and long-lasting impressions on their students" (p. 17).

How Read-Alouds Are Effective for Middle and High School Students

Middle and high school students enjoy hearing read-alouds, too, yet we seldom think to include them in our instruction. One teacher wrote in her journal how she enjoyed read-alouds when exposed to them in high school:

> I did not experience the joy of being read aloud to until the 11th grade. My English teacher brought stories to life. When he read *The Adventures of Tom Sawyer* to us, he gave each character a personality beyond the words. His style of reading and the fact that he read aloud brought excitement into my life that I had not felt since the first grade.

I used read-alouds as a regular part of my teaching to high school students:

> Read-alouds provided me with an opportunity to model the many different purposes of reading. I could demonstrate the variety of resources that readers use daily, the pleasure readers draw from the activity, and the volume of information that is available in books. (Richardson, 1996, p. 114)

Read-alouds model expressive, enthusiastic reading, transmit the pleasure of reading, and invite listeners to be readers. They are an effective means to promote reading. Another teacher wrote, "It is not just what you read but the teaching strategy that is modeled that makes an impact." Read-alouds make good sense and are just plain fun.

Why Read-Aloud in Content Classes?

Read-alouds should not be reserved only for the English and language arts classes because learners discover information in a variety of situations. Learning becomes more relevant and exciting when fresh approaches such as read-alouds are infused into all content instruction. One has only to read results of any U.S. national testing of adolescents to realize that their reading profile shows only modest gains from middle to high school.

> [A]chievement growth over the high school years is relatively modest compared to the range of achievement that exists at the beginning of high school. Achievement of 12th-graders as a group is not dissimilar to the achievement of 8th graders. (National Center for Educational Statistics, 1997)

Adolescents seem to lack critical reading skills and do little leisure reading. Recent studies have indicated that when adolescents increase their pleasure reading, their literacy profile and performance also increase in academic work (Baumann & Duffy, 1997). If secondary teachers were to read aloud often in their classes, they would expose their students to many messages: Teachers like to read a wide variety of materials; teachers enjoy their students and want to share this reading with them; teachers see connections between content topics and pleasure reading; and teachers show students how to be expressive readers.

Principles for Selecting and Using Read-Alouds

To ensure that read-alouds are used wisely and to their greatest effect in the content classroom, apply the following principles when making selections:

1. The selection should "tie reading to pleasure, not pain" (Chandler, 1997). Selections for read-alouds can be found while reading for pleasure, which is pure serendipity. If you do not enjoy the selection, why would your students? You want them to enjoy the excerpt just as much as you have and then to read the rest of the selection for themselves. Introducing the selection via a read-aloud in a content class is a way of linking pleasure and learning, not inducing boredom or pain. Read-alouds are a "treat" or break from a lecture approach. For instance, while reading *The Butcher's Theater* (Kellerman, 1988), I was simply enjoying a mystery for leisure reading. I felt Avi's frustration as he tried to check through files and kept losing his place. This gave me insight about what it might be like to have a learning disability, so I shared the insight with my students. (Chapter 8 will tell you how.)

2. The selection should encourage discussion and application of content material. Authors write to stimulate thinking and to encourage the reader to consider another way of viewing the world. Ask yourself if the selection that you enjoy so much will also encourage your students to think, question, and apply. For example, teaching poetry was always a challenge for me as an English teacher, because my students resisted discussing poetry. So when a colleague told me about Anastasia's terrible experience with poetry in *Anastasia Krupnik* (Lowry, 1979), I had to read the novel. I then followed his suggestion and used passages from it for a read-aloud, and discovered that a lively discussion about poetry was possible with high school students. Furthermore, the read-aloud stimulated students to generate characteristics of poetry and apply them to poems during the remaining year. (Chapter 5 explains how to use this read-aloud to teach poetry.)

3. The selection should make the content "come alive." Any topic can be incredibly interesting or intensely dull. Dillard's experience with the frog and the giant water bug in *Pilgram at Tinker Creek* (1974) took my breath away. I read it aloud to my son and he loved it. When I shared it with my colleague in science education, he amazed me with how the passage links to the study of digestion and enzymes. I would never have expected that learning about enzymes would seem so alive to me. (Chapter 2 describes this section.)

4. The selection should encourage further reading and inquiry. Read-alouds in the classroom should show that reading really can expand horizons. Students will explore more about topics that are only mentioned in the classroom. After all, textbooks are really secondary resources, just as encyclopedias are. Textbook authors may have read the original or primary resources, but they condense the information into compact resources. A read-aloud can show a primary source, and expand students' awareness about the condensed information. After reading Teper's (1987) *After Long Silence*, I wanted to read more about music and its effect on listeners. I had never realized that musicians deliberately choose chords to "tune" my mood. (See Chapter 6 about using this selection.)

How to Locate Great Read-Alouds

Read-alouds help teachers start the conversations that lead to understandings about reading and writing to learn. Authors of literature are good at what they do precisely because they possess an intuitive knowledge of the human condition. They know about the pain and joy of life, and their gift for expression commands the reader's interest and attention. Authors often indirectly provide teachers with the very best introductions to their content. Although authors may not have studied math to the extent

teachers have, they realize how math applies in life and convey it in vignettes that lead to interesting discussions.

How do teachers locate read-alouds? Not in any studied fashion. Read voraciously. Read all types of books. Read for pleasure. Read simply for learning and pleasure and the read-alouds will be obvious. Keep reading for pleasure as the main goal, not reading for instructional opportunities. Those opportunities will come, but first, have fun. If you find a read-aloud while reading for pleasure, your students will realize this and know that you are giving them a treat. The goal is to associate the pleasurable experience of the read-aloud with increased opportunities for learning. Do not read for your students, but keep them and the content in mind as you read. The possibilities will begin to jump at you.

If you are not an avid reader, select material that interests you and begin reading small pieces a few days a week. Be sure to make time in your schedule for reading. Even on busy days, try for 15 minutes of pleasure reading before bedtime.

Vary the types of material you read. I used to read only prose and skim the newspaper. Over time, I discovered that journalistic writing can be fascinating. Chatwin's (1987) *The Songlines*, about Australian Aboriginals, and *Pilgrim at Tinker Creek*, about the author's observations of nature, have entertained while teaching me. I now read the newspaper much more completely. When I visited Russia, the tourist guidebooks provided me with a wealth of information, which inspired me to read historical accounts and to search for Russian writers who are less well-known in the Western world. Do not limit your reading.

Share your selections with other teachers. They often have insights and instructional possibilities to share about particular selections. Many of the instructional suggestions in this book have come from my colleagues. Read all genres of literature. Read contemporary adult literature, as well as children's and adolescent literature. My read-alouds come from my own reading, which sometimes includes good literature for children and adolescents, but is often adult oriented. I also enjoy mysteries and informational books. If you read widely, you will be better equipped to introduce students to a wide variety of literature.

Share with your students resources they will read for years to come, for instance, classics such as *The Phantom Tollbooth* or *Anastasia Krupnik*. Introduce them to authors such as Mark Twain, who had a surprising knowledge of algebra (see Chapter 3), or Dumas, who provides innovative reasons to learn a foreign language (see Chapter 7).

To introduce read-alouds in your classroom, begin with the examples in this book. However, your best collection will come from your own reading and sharing your personal pleasure and excitement, which you then can transmit to your students.

Read-Alouds for Science

2

In science there are three important aspects of learning: *habits of mind, knowledge as product,* and *thinking skills as process. Habits of mind* is the curiosity and creativity that the study of science can spark. Each of the read-alouds in this chapter has generated curiosity and a creative way of viewing science topics. *Knowledge as product* refers to the information to be learned in the study of science. The selections in this chapter provide much information and stimulate the learner to seek more knowledge. *Thinking skills as process* may be the most important area a scientist develops, because the skills influence the way a scientist proceeds with a study. In this chapter, several suggestions for thinking skills related to the read-aloud topics are provided. The selections include a best-selling novel, a nonfiction journalistic account, a factual account, and a biographical account.

Selection 1: Observing Nature

The selection on page 9 is an excerpt from the Pulitzer Prize winning, *Pilgrim at Tinker Creek*, in which Anne Dillard explores her environment and writes as we see through her eyes. Most readers cannot catch their breath for a moment after reading this passage, any more than the author could after observing the event. This is journalistic writing at its best. This selection creates an environment for curiosity, a longing to know. It has a "blood and guts" quality that captures students' interest; they want to pay attention.

Activities for Nature Studies

This selection from *Pilgram at Tinker Creek* motivates students to want to learn more about its topic and gives them a reason to learn. It is a springboard to knowledge acquisition; therefore, it enhances *habits of mind*.

Several topics could be pursued as a result of this reading. Some students will want to find out more about frogs: What are their habits? Some students will want to research giant water bugs: Do they ever attack people? Do they live where I live? Under what conditions do they thrive? What is their origin? What do they look like? As an introduction to the topic of enzymes, this piece is a rich resource: How does dissolving occur? How do enzymes aid digestion? Are enzymes important to human beings? Is there an analogy between how humans digest food with enzymes in the mouth and how the water bug dissolves its prey?

Thinking skills as process are used also in this piece. The author used process skills to learn about the environment during a real-life event. She learned about her surroundings by becoming a skillful observer. Students understand real reasons to observe from her model of careful observation. Pose the following questions to begin the thinking process: Why do frogs seem to wait until the last minute to take off? Why was she more amazed and dumbstruck than startled? Why would she be walking around the creek? Inferential thinking and subsequent reading to find answers also will occur as a result of such questions.

Connecting Language Arts and Nature

From a language arts perspective, this piece is a model for writing, both process and product. The author keeps a journal, carries it with her, and jots down what she sees. This leads to later reflection and rewriting for an audience. She goes from notes scribbled in a journal to such rich language: "His very skull seemed to collapse and settle like a kicked tent...watched the taut, glistening skin on his shoulders ruck, rumble, and fall." It is doubtful that Dillard jotted down those exact words in her first entry. Instead, she thought, reread, and revisited the scene until just the right words could be found and used to pull in her reader. By reading the passage aloud to secondary biology students, the teacher is a reading model: The teacher is expressive and enthusiastic. The teacher enjoys a variety of writing. Reading is enjoyment, a way to learn, and a way to share.

Send students to observe their own part of the school grounds or to their favorite hiding and exploring places in the community, with a clipboard, paper, and pencil. The students may see a few ants, a frog, or a dandelion. Instruct them to be still, with their eyes open, and observe. Ask them to take notes and describe

Read-Aloud from *Pilgrim at Tinker Creek*

A couple of summers ago I was walking along the edge of the island to see what I could see in the water, and mainly to scare frogs. Frogs have an inelegant way of taking off from invisible positions on the bank just ahead of your feet, in dire panic, emitting a froggy 'yike!' and splashing into the water. Incredibly, this amused me, and, incredibly, it amuses me still. As I walked along the grassy edge of the island, I got better and better at seeing frogs both in and out of the water. I learned to recognize, slowing down, the difference in texture of the light reflected from mudbank, water, grass, or frog. Frogs were flying all around me. At the end of the island I noticed a small green frog. He was exactly half in and half out of the water, looking like a schematic diagram of an amphibian, and he didn't jump.

He didn't jump; I crept closer. At last I knelt on the island's winterkilled grass, lost, dumbstruck, staring at the frog in the creek just four feet away. He was a very small frog with wide, dull eyes. And just as I looked at him, he slowly crumpled and began to sag. The spirit vanished from his eyes as if snuffed. His skin emptied and drooped; his very skull seemed to collapse and settle like a kicked tent. He was shrinking before my eyes like a deflating football. I watched the taut, glistening skin on his shoulders ruck, and rumple, and fall. Soon, part of his skin, formless as a pricked balloon, lay in floating folds like bright scum on top of the water: it was a monstrous and terrifying thing. I gaped bewildered, appalled. An oval shadow hung in the water behind the drained frog; then the shadow glided away. The frog skin bag started to sink.

I had read about the giant water bug, but had never seen one. *Giant water bug* is really the name of the creature, which is an enormous, heavy-bodied brown beetle. It eats insects, tadpoles, fish, and frogs. Its grasping forelegs are mighty and hooked inward. It seizes a victim with these legs, hugs it tight, and paralyzes it with enzymes injected during a vicious bite. That one bite is the only bite it ever takes. Through the puncture shoot the poisons that dissolve the victim's muscles and bones and organs—all but the skin—and through it the giant water bug sucks out the victim's body, reduced to a juice. This event is quite common in warm fresh water. The frog I saw was being sucked by a giant water bug. I had been kneeling on the island grass; when the unrecognizable flap of frog skin settled on the creek bottom, swaying, I stood up and brushed the knees of my pants. I couldn't catch my breath. (pp. 13–14) what was seen. Have them try to capture the reader with descriptions and make the reader want to learn more.

Selection 2: Nonfiction for Environmental Studies

"Nonfiction is it! The answer! It's the way to go when trying to hook middle school readers. Nonfiction accommodates the wide variety of skill and interest levels we see in our classrooms," says one teacher, who uses Christopher Lampton's (1988) *Endangered Species* with her students. Whenever she promotes nonfiction reading to teachers, she is "struck by the power and simplicity of reading aloud. Perhaps, because it is such an obvious activity, it is often overlooked by many of us who are eager to bring high-tech, smoke and mirrors to our lessons."

Lampton's best stories are presented in his chapter, "How Species Became Extinct," about the dodo bird and the passenger pigeon. The dodo bird was found

Read-Aloud From *Endangered Species*

The day of the Pleistocene hunter is long gone, but humans still hunt—for food, for sport, and for animal by-products such as furs and oils....

The most spectacular example of an animal hunted to extinction—since the Pleistocene, anyway—occurred within the memory of people alive today. The victim was the passenger pigeon, once the most common bird in North America, and possibly the most common bird on Earth....

When the settlers arrived on the continent...the total population of passenger pigeons was certainly in the billions, and they migrated northward and southward across the continent in flocks of more than 100 million birds. When they flew across the sky, the sun would vanish, and night would seem to fall....

Obviously, the passenger pigeon was a successful species, well adapted to its environment. But, in a world dominated by human beings, it had made a crucial evolutionary mistake: it was delicious to eat....

The birds had not evolved to resist that modern weapon of destruction, the gun....

No one knows when the slaughter of the passenger pigeon began...but the end of the slaughter is quite easy to pinpoint. On March 24, 1900, a young hunter shot the last passenger pigeon ever seen in the wild. (pp. 26–28)

[From *Endangered Species* by Christopher Lampton. Copyright ©1988. Reprinted with permission of Grolier.]

by sailors on Mauritius, where it had no natural enemies. Because it could not fly, was clumsy and not too intelligent, it had no natural defenses. Sailors just walked up behind it and bashed it to death. The dodo bird was extinct by 1680.

The story about the passenger pigeon in the read-aloud selection, exemplifies the problem of overhunting in endangering species.

Activities for Environmental Studies

This short passage does much to enlighten students to the problem of protecting endangered species while enhancing listening and note taking skills. The extinction described is in moving detail. Reading the passage aloud brings the problem home to the students and makes environmental concerns real. "So that's how it could happen. I never really thought about it," is a common reaction. Because the job of teacher is to make students think about what they would not ordinarily, such comments demonstrate how the read-aloud can broaden horizons.

To sharpen listening skills, instruct students to listen very closely for all clues that make up the explanation of the extinction. The students should not take any notes, but just listen to the read-aloud. Afterward, record on the chalkboard or an overhead projector what the students say they heard. Then reread the selection while students check their notes for accuracy.

Also, have students take the viewpoint of either the hunter or the bird and write stories depicting the bird's extinction using the facts from the read-aloud. Their stories could be shared within the class. After reading this segment aloud, have students brainstorm other examples of extinct animals or plants. Speculation of how the extinction could have occurred would promote lively discussion.

Inquiry projects are a logical extension, with students selecting different species to research. Students might investigate different theories about the extinction of a number of species. Lampton's chapter titles pose other questions that might become the start for research.

This read-aloud could provide the opportunity for a debate about the rights of hunters versus the rights of species. For such a debate to work effectively, be careful not to give away your own opinions too early. Controversial issues always have at least two sides, but no single resolution. However, such debate offers more opportunities for research: What kind of shot, lead or steel, might be best for hunters to use? (Lead shot poisons animals so steel shot may be a better alternative. For example, condors that had been carefully bred in captivity to increase their numbers died when released to the wild because they ate other animals killed with lead shot.)

Another area of endangered species is plants. A classic example is the Ginkgo tree, thought to be extinct, but rediscovered growing in a remote area of China. This Asian tree with fan-shaped leaves has been reintroduced in the United States and can now be found growing all over (much to the dismay of those who step on the fruit of the female tree leaves).

Other questions that could arise from this read-aloud are: What practices have led to a species of animal or plant becoming endangered? What other animals or plants have become extinct or been placed on an endangered list? What are the characteristics of an endangered species? Are there levels of endangerment? What practices have led to removing a plant or animal from an endangered list?

During one month, students could be on the lookout for news stories about possible endangered species. A collage or bulletin board could display these findings.

Make time for book talks and read-alouds in the classroom as often as possible. Encourage reading about science just for fun, which can lead to not only a deeper appreciation of literature but to the garnering of a great deal of information as well. For instance, there are many trade books that provide fascinating tidbits beyond the textbook information, such as the fact that butterflies have taste buds on their feet. Discovering such interesting facts in enjoyable books could lead a student to question further, read more, and eventually be ready— even eager—to write a term paper.

Selection 3: Launching Into Space

Astronomy can be one of the most abstract units in science. To make the unit more concrete and personal, read aloud from R. Mike Mullane's (1996) *Lift Off! An Astronaut's Dream*, a nonfiction account of a space-shuttle launch and mission. The 96-page book is easy to read and is written in a friendly style. Mullane describes the mission and his role, and he provides autobiographical background about his desire to become an astronaut. He addresses some interesting facts that can pique students' interests. Most of us do not realize that the astronauts must wear diapers; of course, such a fact not only heightens interest, but also qualifies as "gross" enough to entertain teenagers.

Activities for Astronomy

Astronomy includes the study of the sun, the stars, and the planets, as well as space exploration. This read-aloud has several applications for space exploration. Students have many questions about space travel that may be difficult to answer: How are space flights made? What does lift off feel like? What precautions should be taken? Mullane's descriptions of what the space shuttle is like, how the bathroom and kitchen are configured, how one eats while in space, and the ways in which astronauts amuse themselves, can help answer such questions.

Read-Aloud From *Lift-Off! An Astronaut's Dream*

"*Atlantis*, the weather plane is making one last check of some clouds, and as soon as the pilot gives us a clearance, we'll continue with the countdown."

The commander answers the launch director's call. "Roger. We're ready."

I'm mission specialist 1...ready for my second ride into space. I'm also miserable. I wiggle in my seat to try to get comfortable, but it's impossible. I have eighty-five pounds of equipment wrapped around my body...and...straps...holding me tightly to the steel chair. The space shuttle seats are not couches like the ones...in the old days of the space program. Then, there were just a few astronauts. Now, there are many, and it would be too expensive to build separate couches for all their different sizes. So the seats are all the same, just flat plates of heavy steel with thin cushions...I've been lying in mine for the past four hours waiting for the weather to clear....

And the diaper I'm wearing is soaked! Yes! A diaper!...Actually, there are three times when an astronaut has to wear a diaper: during launch, during reentry, and during a space walk....

"*Atlantis*, the weather pilot just reported that the clouds are no longer a problem. We'll be coming out of the hold in five seconds...four...three...two...one... T-minus nine minutes and counting."

I silently shout for joy. Finally, we're counting down to launch! (pp. 3–5)

[From *Lift Off! An Astronaut's Dream* by R. Mike Mullane. Copyright ©1995 by Silver Burdett Press. Reprinted with permission of Macmillan General Reference, a division of Ahsoug.]

To create their own solar system, Mullane writes about how the astronauts squirted a blob of orange juice into the air, where it floated weightlessly as a ball. Then, using colored candies, the astronauts placed planets around this sun. Mercury was a red candy, Venus a yellow, and Earth a green (pp. 51–52). Encourage students to make their own solar systems with creative props. Ask them, What does Earth look like from space? Mullane points out that astronauts do not watch television while in space; they watch the earth. He describes his view. From his description and other resources, have students illustrate their own views of Earth from space.

What is an aurora? How is one formed? Mullane sees one from space and explains the formation. How much radiation are astronauts exposed to in space? A human skull willed to science travels with the astronauts on this trip. From it, doctors will determine how much space radiation penetrates an astronaut's skull, and then they will design protective shields. Students can be encouraged to locate more information about these issues, either in their textbooks, from primary resources, or through the Internet.

To reinforce the read-aloud and discussion of space exploration, encourage students to look around their own homes for evidence of space explorations. What do we use in everyday life as a result of space missions? The telephone and television use long-distance signals relayed through satellite stations. We receive satellite transmissions of the weather. Pens that write when held at any angle are the direct result of a need in weightless space. Medical technology has advanced as a result of experiments aboard mission shuttles. Instant foods—not just the freeze-dried variety—also resulted from needs in space.

Connecting Language Arts and Astronomy

One of the stylistic qualities of *Lift Off!* is the manner in which the author begins chapters with an engaging event or example—a "mind grabber." He places the reader in the space shuttle during the event, explaining important facts. He looks back at himself as a child, recounting segments of his personal journey to becoming an astronaut. This mixture of autobiography, fact, and journalism works to keep a reader attentive. Have students indicate where

and how the author intersperses information with interesting scenes. Encourage them to look for similar examples in other books, and to use this technique in their own writing.

Mullane switches between first, second, and third person, depending on his emphasis. To describe actual events, he writes in third person; to describe how he felt, he writes in first person. When writing specifically to encourage young people, the author switches to second person. His advice is palatable to teenagers within the context of the story: "You need an education.... What's the most important subject to study? That's an easy one. Reading. If you can't read, your education stops. You can't study math, history, science, or anything else. You must be a good reader for a dream to come true!" (pp. 88–89). Point out to students that writers consciously make decisions about voice based on what they intend to write and on their audience. Ask students to find specific examples of how the author does this.

As Mullane describes the selection and training processes for astronauts, he provides an opportunity to discuss career orientations. Have students brainstorm about what courses would be necessary to become an astronaut, which could lead to discussions about other types of careers, the qualities necessary for a career, as well as what background is necessary for a specific career in space.

A major message in *Lift Off!* is how one can turn a personal dream into reality through hard work. Using Mullane's autobiographical account as a starting point, encourage students to think of other individuals who had a dream that influenced their life direction. Using these examples, have students write an essay about one of these individuals or about themselves and their personal dreams.

Mullane comments that a beam of light he observes in space is thousands of years old before it reaches Earth. "What would it have been like to have streaked through trillions and trillions of miles of black space?" he ponders (p. 25). To introduce writing, invite students to become ghost writers, describing the life of such a beam of light. Or, a student might become a satellite in orbit. What would the satellite have to do to broadcast a phone call? Would it be worried about colliding with a meteor? Even though the essay would be fiction, have students research facts to create a plausible scenario.

Brief Selections for Science

An Unexpected Journalist

Charles Frazier's (1997) *Cold Mountain* won acclaim as the National Book Foundation winner and top bestseller in 1997. A soldier deserts the confederate army and walks home to Cold Mountain. His journey shows readers another side of the U.S. Civil War—no glamour here, no glory—just people trying to make a living in very hard times.

On many occasions, the soldier is surprised by the kindness of strangers. One time, he is taken in by a shriveled old woman who lives as a hermit in the hills. She knows how to treat the soldier's illness by using natural remedies. One day, he looks inside her makeshift home and discovers that she is more educated than she had first seemed:

> He looked about the desk at the papers. He picked up a journal and opened it to a drawing of goats. They had eyes and feet on them like people, and the sentences of the entry below were hard to parse, but they seemed to contrast the behavior of certain goats on cold days to their behavior on hot. Inman leafed through farther and found pictures of plants and then more pictures of goats in every *imaginable attitude*, all done in a mute and limited palette, as if she painted with clothes dye. Inman read the stories that went with the pictures, and they told of what the goats ate and how they acted toward each other and what moods seized them from day to day. It seemed to Inman that the woman's aim was to list in every detail the habits of their culture. (p. 222)

As with the Dillard selection, this one provides an opportunity to discuss with students the processes a scientist uses to learn. The old woman has detailed the behavior of her goats as she has observed them carefully over time. She is a skillful observer of her surroundings with a real reason to observe.

A stimulating assignment might be for students to observe animals they care about for a period of time, noting and writing down various habits and patterns. This exercise creates a habit of mind, while generating new knowledge.

Of Chemicals, Chemistry, and Preserving Insects

Annie Dillard, author of the first selection in this chapter, also wrote *An American Childhood* (1990), a series of stories about her early life experiences. One story involved collecting insects:

> To collect insects I equipped myself with the usual paraphernalia: glass-headed pins, a net, and a killing jar.... I knew, I thought, what I was doing. In the bottom of the killing jar—formerly a pickle jar—I laid a wad of cotton soaked in cleaning fluid containing carbon tetrachloride, which compound I thrilled myself by calling, offhandedly, 'carbon tet.'...After a suitable interval I poured out the dead thing as carefully as I could, and pinned it...in a cigar box."
>
> (She leaves the bug collection and looks at it again 4 weeks later.)...I found a rhinoceros beetle crawling on its pin. (pp. 443–444)

Dillard used carbon tetrachloride, a cleaning fluid and spot remover, to kill and preserve insects. Chloride, which affects enzymes in the liver, acts as a general anesthetic. After it had dried, the insects would be revived, which Dillard discovered in an unappealing way. Because it damages the ozone, "carbon tet" is seldom used today for the purpose of preserving insects.

This passage could stimulate discussion in a chemistry class about the effectiveness of chemicals for certain tasks. What would be used today to preserve insects? Why? What other chemicals have common uses? Why are some chemicals destructive to the environment?

Conclusion

Although you would not expect to learn about science while reading for pleasure, the selections in this chapter presented much scientific information: how chemicals affect enzymes, the importance of observation, extinction of species, exploration in space and its effects on Earth, healing properties of plants, the scientific method of inquiry, and the importance of using the right chemical solutions. I learned about giant water bugs, how two species became extinct, that space exploration is classified as astronomy and about its impact on my daily life.

Through these read-alouds, I discovered new and fascinating ways to illustrate for students the power of language—that it is important to use the right word and find the right metaphor, and how voice can change readers' perspectives.

The read-alouds show the care the authors have taken with their final products, which helps students see that the art of writing requires careful attention but is rewarded by knowing that readers are provided with enjoyable, entertaining, and thought-provoking material.

Read-Alouds for Mathematics and Geography

3

"**H**ow can I teach reading in my math class without getting away from the math material I'm supposed to teach?" This question came from a collection of "nightmares"Bintz (1997, p. 2) collected from content teachers. Pressure to cover the content is a teacher nightmare and can become a student nightmare as well. All are rushing toward their goals, and the pleasure of learning is forgotten or relegated to last place. When teachers use read-alouds that correlate with the instruction, the nightmare can become a pleasant dream.

How can a teacher use literature in math? In response to a need for reforms in teaching and learning mathematics, the Curriculum and Evaluation Standards for School Mathematics (1989) identified several components of a new math program: (1) learning to value mathematics, (2) becoming confident in one's own ability, (3) becoming a mathematical problem solver, (4) learning to communicate mathematically, and (5) learning to reason mathematically. Using literature that refers to mathematics topics can enhance the value of learning mathematics, instill confidence in ability and problem solving, and stimulate communications and reasoning skills. At the same time, the *Professional Standards for Teaching Mathematics* (1991) focused on the following: (1) worthwhile mathematical tasks, (2) conducting discourse, (3) establishing a learning environment, and (4) analysis of teaching and learning. Read-alouds that reflect mathematical tasks will encourage discourse, establish a learning environment, and stimulate analytic learning. In order to foster these goals, the following literature excerpts can be used as read-alouds for math. In several of the read-alouds selected for this chapter, not only is mathematics featured but also geography. Therefore, these connections to geography are explored as the math connections are described. Such connections demonstrate opportunities for thematic learning. The excerpts in this chapter include a best-selling novel, a Mark Twain essay, a fantasy novel, a math activity book by a noted author of mathematics resource books, and a young adult novel.

Selection 1: Calculations and Chess

This selection features an excerpt from Katherine Neville's (1998) best-selling novel, *The Eight*. One of my college students, a mathematics major, recommended *The Eight* to me after I had read aloud another selection in his class. He commented that this novel was one of the few he had read and enjoyed in the past year. He confessed that he did not read much literature but was intrigued and stimulated by the pre-

dominate emphasis on mathematics in the novel. Although the novel is long, he could not put it down. He knew I would like it too, and he was correct.

The plot is a search for the mathematical equation that will result in a formula for immortality. The equation is revealed in a giant chess game, played out over two centuries by different characters, including Catherine the Great. Pieces of the Montglane Chess Service, once owned by Charlemagne, provide the clues. Whoever possesses a chess piece from the Montglane Service plays the game, sometimes unwittingly. Whoever can gather all the pieces and reassemble them into one game can solve the puzzle. The novel is a mystery full of intrigue, historical references, and allusions to geography, philosophy, music, and science, as well as mathematics. The story begins in 1972 with the experiences of Cat (Catherine Velis), a computer expert for an accounting firm, and then it flashes back to 1790.

The Eight will challenge readers with its intricacy, use of language, well-drawn characters, and depth. Teachers will want to read the entire 550-page novel and will find several read-aloud passages for use in many content areas.

Activities for Mathematics

A mathematics teacher might use this read-aloud selection as an introduction to a unit on solving equations. Discussion might be introduced with the question Why do we have equations? The students' responses could lead to insights about mathematics as a form of language used to communicate. Because computer programmers rely on mathematics to communicate, students might also want to investigate computer programs designed to play chess.

Playing chess challenges one's use of mathematics. A player must apply probabilities and logic and use critical thinking skills. A chessboard uses the numbers 64, 32, and 16. Have students explore the relationships among these numbers. Encourage students to explore several problems using a standard chessboard as a point of reference:

1. Determine how many different-sized squares there are on the board and how a square is defined (1×1, 2×2, etc.).

2. After eliminating the top left and bottom right squares on the chessboard, how many domino pieces would it take to cover the remaining squares?

Read-Aloud From *The Eight*

We labored over the puzzle all night. Now I could see why mathematicians felt a transcendental wave of energy washing over them when they discovered a new formula or saw a pattern in something they'd looked at a thousand times. Only in mathematics was there that sense of moving through another dimension, one that didn't exist in time and place—that feeling of falling into and through a puzzle, of having it surround you in a physical way.

I wasn't a great mathematician, but I understood Pythagoras when he said mathematics was one with music. As Lily and Solarin labored over the chess moves on the board and I tried to capture the pattern on paper, I felt as if I could hear the formula of the Montglane Service singing to me. It was like an elixir running through my veins, driving me on with its beautiful harmony as we beat ourselves into the ground trying to find the pattern in the pieces.

It wasn't easy. As Solarin had implied, when you were dealing with a formula comprised of sixty-four squares, thirty-two pieces, and sixteen positions on a cloth, the possible combinations were far more than the total number of stars in the known universe. Though it looked from our drawing as if some of the moves were Knight moves and others Rook or Bishop, we couldn't be sure. The entire pattern had to fit within the sixty-four squares on the board of the Montglane Service.

[From *The Eight* by Katherine Neville. Copyright ©1988. Reprinted with permission of Random House, Ballantine Books.]

3. Given 32 pieces of one color and 32 pieces of another, how many different ways can pieces be arranged on the board? What patterns appear?

This passage can be a stimulus to learn about Pythagoras. Why is he mentioned in this passage? Because Pythagoras said that mathematics is one with music, ask students to think about links between music and mathematics: Where does one find mathematics in music? (The beats, the meters, and the scale notes are based on specific mathematical ratios.)

Connecting Language Arts and Math

From the language arts perspective, this passage provides several metaphors. Can the listener-reader identify them? Neville, like all writers, consciously selects vocabulary that will entice readers. What words most affect the student as a listener-reader? Discuss the metaphors and word choices to demonstrate the integration of listening, reading, and writing.

Formal writing assignments could include having students select a mathematician who has made a significant contribution to the field and write a brief paper about him or her. Writing journal entries or formal essays could include answering the following questions:

Is there a significance of the number 8 to mathematics? To chess? To this novel?

Have you ever been close to solving a math problem and spent much longer than you intended to solve it?

How do you feel when you solve a math problem? Are you elated, thankful to be finished, or do you think about other methods you could have used to find a solution?

How many times have you studied a problem, abandoned it and returned, and suddenly found a solution that you could not before?

Reading assignments could include having students read a novel by an author who uses mathematics and science as a basis for the story. Many science fiction writers, including Isaac Asimov and Mary Gentle, use parallel dimensions and mathematical equations.

Have students locate a newspaper article, past or current, that reports a mathematical discovery. How can this discovery affect people?

Selection 2: Algebra, Geography, and the Mississippi River

The read-aloud from Mark Twain's (1917) *Life On the Mississippi* was suggested by a teacher who first used the chapter "Cut-Offs and Stephen" while teaching an interdisciplinary course in earth science and geography. At the time, he was reading Twain's book for his own enjoyment. Later, while teaching about linear equations in an algebra class, he remembered this read-aloud and thought it would be a good way to bring literature into the study of both math and geography. His class was working on applying the concept of linear equations to real life relations, such as height and shoe size. Students, enjoyed Twain's humorous use of math.

In the selection on pages 22–23, Twain, a noted expert on the Mississippi River, discusses "one of the Mississippi's oddest peculiarities—that of shortening its length from time to time" (p. 153). He discusses the many horseshoe curves in the river, which have been altered over time due not only to acts of nature such as flooding, but also to acts of men, who are likely to "cut a little gutter across the narrow neck of land some dark night" (p. 154) and thus change the course of the river so that it flows by their property.

Twain was a humorist not a mathematician. Could his calculations possibly have been correct? The teacher calculated the slope of the line Twain had described in his text. He then graphed it as he had done other problems in his algebra class. Much to his surprise, the calculations were precise. Twain had apparently done the math himself to come up with the figures.

The teacher's graph (see page 24) shows the slope of the line with the y axis representing distance in 100-mile increments, and the x axis representing time in 100 year increments. The line intersects the x axis at about 740, suggesting that about 740 years from the time of Twain's writing, the length of the river from Cairo, Illinois, to New Orleans, Louisiana, would have been zero, almost the same prediction Twain made. The figures on the graph are labeled to identify the formula for slope, which is how the teacher was able to apply Twain's figures to the graph. Twain provided all the numbers to be used in the calculations. The graph led to a better understanding by students of how algebra is used in the real world.

Activities for Algebra

Certainly, sharing this read-aloud when teaching slope can make the abstract more concrete. Using the graph, students will begin to understand that slope always reflects the relationship of one variable to another (the change in the length of the river in miles per year or the change in distance over time).

Following this application, students can look at scaled drawings and pick two points on a map. This is a perfect opportunity to learn how to read a mileage chart on a map. Once the scale factor is known, they can plot the straightest path between those two points. Because the straightest path is not always the traveled path, students can use geography to decide on possible routes.

The notion of prediction can be discussed: whether just "knowing facts" as Twain did can account for all the factors involved in a prediction or whether other factors must be taken into account. Is it likely that the river was ever so long

Read-Aloud From *Cut-Offs and Stephen*

These dry details are of importance in one particular. They give me an opportunity of introducing one of the Mississippi's oddest peculiarities—that of shortening its length from time to time. If you will throw a long, pliant apple-paring over your shoulder, it will pretty fairly shape itself into an average section of the Mississippi River; that is, the nine or ten hundred miles stretching from Cairo, Illinois, southward to New Orleans, the same being wonderfully crooked, with a brief straight bit here and there at wide intervals. The two-hundred-mile stretch from Cairo northward to St. Louis is by no means so crooked, that being a rocky country which the river cannot cut much.

The water cuts the alluvial banks of the "lower" river into deep horseshoe curves; so deep, indeed, that in some places if you were to get ashore at one extremity of the horseshoe and walk across the neck, half or three-quarters of a mile, you could sit down and rest a couple of hours while your steamer was coming around the long elbow at a speed of ten miles an hour to take you on board again. When the river is rising fast, some scoundrel whose plantation is back in the country, and therefore of inferior value, has only to watch his chance, cut a little gutter across the narrow neck of land some dark night, and turn the water into it, and in a wonderfully short time a miracle has happened: to wit, the whole Mississippi has taken possession of that little ditch, and placed the countryman's plantation on its bank (quadrupling its value), and that other party's formerly valuable plantation finds itself away out yonder on a big island; the old watercourse around it will soon shoal up, boats cannot approach within ten miles of it, and down goes its value to a fourth of its former worth. Watches are kept on those narrow necks at needful times, and if a man happens to be caught cutting a ditch across them, the chances are all against his ever having another opportunity to cut a ditch.

Pray observe some of the effects of this ditching business. Once there was a neck opposite Port Hudson, Louisiana, which was only half a mile across in its narrowest place. You could walk across there in fifteen minutes; but if you made the journey around the cape on a raft, you traveled thirty-five miles to accomplish the same thing. In 1722 the river darted through that neck, deserted its old bed, and thus shortened itself thirty-five miles. In the same way it shortened itself twenty-five miles at Black Hawk Point in 1699. Below Red River Landing, Raccourci cut-off was made (forty or fifty years ago, I think). This shortened the river twenty-eight miles. In our day, if you travel by river from the southernmost of these three cut-offs to

(continued)

the northernmost, you go only seventy miles. To do the same thing a hundred and seventy-six years ago, one had to go a hundred and fifty-eight miles—a shortening of eighty-eight miles in that trifling distance. At some forgotten time in the past, cut-offs were made above Vidalia, Louisiana, at Island 92, at Island 84, and at Hale's Point. These shortened the river, in the aggregate, seventy-seven miles.

Since my own day on the Mississippi, cut-offs have been made at Hurricane Island, at Island 100, at Napoleon, Arkansas, at Walnut Bend, and at Council Bend. These shortened the river, in the aggregate, sixty-seven miles. In my own time a cut off was made at American Bend, which shortened the river ten miles or more.

Therefore the Mississippi between Cairo and New Orleans was twelve hundred and fifteen miles long one hundred and seventy-six years ago. It was eleven hundred and eighty after the cut-off of 1722. It was one thousand and forty after the American Bend cut-off. It has lost sixty-seven miles since. Consequently, its length is only nine-hundred and seventy-three miles at present.

Now, if I wanted to be one of those ponderous scientific people, and "let on" to prove what had occurred in the remote past by what had occurred in a given time in the recent past, or what will occur in the far future by what has occurred in late years, what an opportunity is here! Geology never had such a chance, nor such exact data to argue from! Nor "development of species," either! Glacial epochs are great things, but they are vague—vague. Please observe:

In the space of one hundred and seventy-six years the Lower Mississippi has shortened itself two hundred and forty-two miles. That is an average of a trifle over one mile and a third per year. Therefore, any calm person, who is not blind or idiotic, can see that in the Old Oolitic Silurian Period, just a million years ago next November, the Lower Mississippi River was upward of one million three hundred thousand miles long, and stuck out over the Gulf of Mexico like a fishing-rod. And by the same token any person can see that seven hundred and forty-two years from now the Lower Mississippi will be only a mile and three-quarters long, and Cairo and New Orleans will have joined their streets together, and be plodding comfortably along under a single mayor and a mutual board of aldermen. There is something fascinating about science. One gets such wholesale returns of conjecture out of such a trifling investment of fact. (pp. 153–156)

[From *Life on the Mississippi* by Mark Twain (1917). New York: Harper & Row.]

Mississippi River graph for teaching slope

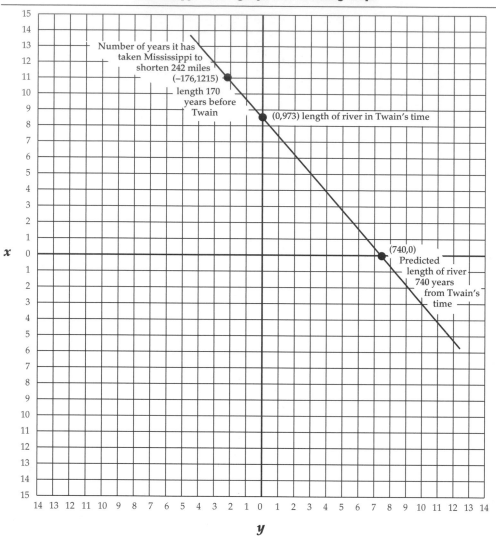

Note: Each block = 100 units; the *x*-axis represents time in 100-year increments, and the *y*-axis represents distance in 100-mile increments.

Standard formula for finding slope
m = change in *y* divided by change in *x*.

$m = \dfrac{y_2 - y_1}{x_2 - x_1}$ change in distance (miles)
change in time (years)

$m = \dfrac{973 - 1215}{0 - 176}$

$m = \dfrac{-242}{176}$ distance river had shortened
time it took

$m = -1.375$ average change in river size per year

Formula for predicting length of river 1 million years ago
$y = mx + b,$ where
$x =$ time in 100-year increments, or $-(10^6)$ years
$b =$ length of river at time of Twain's calcula-tion, or 973 miles
$y = -1.375\,(-[10^6]) + 973$
$y = 1,375,000 + 973$
$y = 1,375,973$ miles long

[Source: Forget, M.A. (1996). A read-aloud for algebra and geography, by Judy S. Richardson and Mark A. Forget, *Journal of Adolescent & Adult Literacy, 39*(4).]

that it "stuck out over the Gulf of Mexico like a fishing rod" (p. 156)? Is it likely that the river will ever be so short that "Cairo and New Orleans will have joined streets" (p. 156)? Using the literal and inferential levels of comprehension at its best is critical thinking.

Activities for Geography

Activities to teach geography are abundant. An introduction to maps of different kinds and different views would be interesting. Students could look at a map from an atlas in order to see the big picture—the points of Cairo, Illinois, to New Orleans, Louisiana. A close-up view of a road map would show state borders such as Arkansas–Mississippi where the horseshoe curves of the river are detailed. Students could locate specific points Twain writes of such as Red River Landing. A gazetteer would provide details of the very points Twain mentions, and topographical maps would show the relationships of river bank to river and curves to straight lines. Comparing ancient maps to modern ones would show how the land has changed.

Connecting Algebra, Geography, and Language Arts

The paragraph of this excerpt describes how plantation owners seized the opportunity of "locating" their plantations on the river bank. As a possible writing assignment students might write about one of the horseshoe curves Twain describes and how a man might "watch his chance" and make a miracle. How could it be possible to change the curve of the river—how did some plantation owners seize this opportunity—and why might he never again have another opportunity to cut such a ditch?

By locating the numbers Twain quotes and identifying what each number represents in the formula for slope, students are using reading to solve a problem. Have students research and write their own humorous essay to be molded into a preposterous but fact-based word problem, which would be a good way to expand on Twain's exaggerated use of relationships. Such an activity can teach not only about word problems but also an appreciation of the humor in dry wit.

To build vocabulary, have students notice how Twain uses words. What does *alluvial* mean and why is it a good choice (p. 153)? How are glacial epochs "great things but vague" (p. 155)?

Selection 3: An Analogy for Math Terms

From sixth grade on, particularly in the study of geometry, students will encounter the word *circumference*. Most of us describe a *circumference* as being the distance around a circle. Therefore, if we were to read a word spelled *circumfence*, we would most likely do a double-take and reread it to make sure of what we saw. Once we had confirmed that we really saw *circumfence*, we would probably dismiss it as a misspelling. These reactions would surely please Terry Pratchett, author of *The Colour of Magic* (1983).

The *Colour of Magic* is the first novel in Pratchett's science fiction–fantasy series entitled Discworld, which I discovered on a summer holiday in England. I bought a figurine of an intellectual witch precariously balancing a pile of books, and the saleswoman told me that it represented a character in the Discworld series.

The Discworld is a world in the shape of a disc. Characters on Discworld include wizards, trolls, dragons, dwarves, and witches. Great A'tuin the Turtle carries it through the interstellar gulf, balancing on his back four elephants who in turn balance Discworld on theirs. Water flows off of the world into the gulf. Pratchett's wonderful sense of humor and amusing situations keep readers alert and off balance.

Rincewind is the hero in *The Colour of Magic*. He has failed at just about everything he has tried to do in life, especially at being a wizard. His companion, Twoflower, seems innocent and oblivious to danger. Twoflower's desire to experience life leads him and Rincewind on escapades, which he thoroughly enjoys, but Rincewind would just as soon forego. One involves the two of them nearly running off the edge of their world at the Rimfall.

Activities for Math and Geography

Most likely students will have learned by rote the formula for circumference: $p \times d$. However, expressing the concept of circumference is more difficult. This read-aloud selection can help develop a fuller concept. Rinceword's definition is simple and descriptive: "The circumference makes the edge of things." Tethis says that this is also what the circumfence does. After a read-aloud of this passage, have students picture the circumfence, using the description Tethis gives on pages 164–165. Have them draw comparisons of the two problems: Propose the following problems:

If we made a circle with a 30-foot circumference and put a rope around it 10 feet longer than the circumference of the circle, how long would the posts (of equal length) have to be to support the rope?

The distance around other objects is called the perimeter (p). The distance around a circle is called the circumference. What is the origin of meaning for each word? Why are the terms different for basically the same measurement?

We know that p is equal to the circumference divided by the diameter (d). If we took the circumference and diameter measurements of many circles and graphed the ordered pairs of the points, representing these measurements (d, c), what can be said about the graph? (You can then help the students relate p to what they know about the slope of a line.)

Read-Aloud From *The Colour of Magic*

"So why aren't we going over the edge, then?" asked Rincewind with glassy calmness.

"Because your boat hit the Circumfence," said the voice behind him (in tones that made Rincewind imagine submarine chasms and lurking Things in coral reefs).

"The Circumfence?" he repeated.

"Yes. It runs along the edge of the world," said the unseen troll. Above the roar of the waterfall Rincewind thought he could make out the splash of oars. He hoped they were oars.

"Ah, you mean the circumference," said Rincewind. "The circumference makes the edge of things."

"So does the Circumfence," said the troll.

"He means this," said Twoflower, pointing down. Rincewind's eyes followed the finger, dreading what they might see....

Hubwards of the boat was a rope suspended a few feet above the surface of the white water. The boat was attached to it, moored yet mobile, by a complicated arrangement of pulleys and little wooden wheels. They ran along the rope as the unseen rower propelled the craft along the very lip of the Rimfall. That explained one mystery—but what supported the rope?

Rincewind peered along its length and saw a stout wooden post sticking up out of the water a few yards ahead. As he watched, the boat neared it and then passed it, the little wheels clacking neatly around it in a groove obviously cut for the purpose (pp. 160–161).

"All things drift into the Circumfence in time," said the troll, gnomically, gently rocking in his chair. "My job is to recover the flotsam. Timber, of course, and ships. Barrels of wine. Bales of cloth. You."

Light dawned inside Rincewind's head.

"It's a net, isn't it? You've got a net right on the edge of the sea!"

"The Circumfence," nodded the troll. Ripples ran across his chest.

Rincewind looked out into the phosphorescent darkness that surrounded the island, and grinned inanely.

"Of course," he said, "Amazing! You could sink piles and attach it to reefs and—good grief! The net would have to be very strong."

"It is," said Tethis. (pp. 164–165)

[From *The Colour of Magic* by Terry Pratchett. Copyright ©1983. Used with permission of Colin Smythe Limited.]

After such exploration, have students write their own definition of circumference.

Discuss geometric figures in three dimensions, examining the circumference on a sphere, which is the "great circle" in solid geometry. In geography, the equator is the great circle and a circumference. The Tropics of Cancer or Capricorn, although not circumferences, run parallel to the equator. Have students investigate each and how they relate to latitude and longitude. Other interesting questions students might explore are as follows:

How many dollar bills or pound notes would one need, laid end-to-end, to wrap around the circumference of the earth at the Equator?

If you could walk around the Equator, how many steps would you need to take?

Connecting Math, Geography, and Language Arts

This passage provides an excellent opportunity for students to experience what good readers do when confronted with the unexpected in their reading. Just like Rincewind, the reader expects the word to be *circumference*. Readers may pause and reread, thinking they had miscued. When they realize they have not, they will read further to discover clues. We found them immediately, which reassured us that we had read correctly. Good readers expect text to make sense; they reread when it does not; they look for clues to help them understand the context of the material. Discuss these behaviors with students.

Have students write or draw descriptions of this scene or create another scene based on a different geometry term. Story definitions can often make terms more memorable and less rote. Another idea would be to create pairs of words, including the real word and its partner: *circumference* and *circumfence*; *pi* and *pie*. These words could be placed in a "Devil's Dictionary," which contains words that have been created by users to demonstrate knowledge or structural analysis, but are not real words (Cassidy, 1984).

The question of why the term is *circumference* with circles, and it is *perimeter* with other figures may not have a scientific answer. But by looking up the origins for each word, students will discover that both started with Greek and then Latin. *Circum* means around and *ferre* means to bear. *Peri* means around and *metron* means measure. Words have a history and generally carry meaning related to that history.

To demonstrate how much fun playing with words can be, turn to another passage in this book (p. 126), in which one of the characters is commanded to kill two men:

"Both at the same time, or one after the other?" he said.

"Consecutively or concurrently," she assured him.

"What?"

"Just kill them," she said sharply.

Students should enjoy *The Colour of Magic*'s crazy ideas and will relish the world of science fiction.

Brief Selections for Math and Geography

I Hate Math!

For middle schoolers, the alphabetical-probability activity proposed in Marilyn Burns's (1975) *The I Hate Mathematics! Book* is fun to try and quick to read aloud as a way of stimulating problem solving. This activity uses math and engages students in the act of reading— a wonderful combination.

> The letter of the alphabet that occurs most often in written English is the letter *E. T, A, O,* and *N* are the next most frequent. Letters that are used the least are *Q, Z, K, X,* and *J.*
>
> Try it out for yourself. Make up a chart which has a column for each letter. Then pick a page in this book and tally each time a letter appears. (p. 117)

Before actually completing a tally, have students make educated guesses based on probability about the number of times each of the letters might occur on the page of primary, middle, or more challenging level material. This activity can also be done with a computer count, once the pages are typed in. The *Find* feature of a word-processing program will calculate the number of times each letter occurs. Then students could chart occurrences and compare them across the different reading levels of the books analyzed.

Fiction for Problem Solving

In *Catherine, Called Birdy* (1994), by Newbery Award winner Katherine Cushman, the protagonist, Birdy, is a willful teenager who lives in medieval times. This story unfolds through a series of journal entries in which the reader learns about Birdy and her struggles to fit in and grow up, much like middle schoolers struggle to do today. The journal format might inspire middle school students to write down their own day's events and, through writing, problem-solve about life.

One passage in particular demonstrates how easy it is for people to spend all of their money, no matter the era in which they live:

> It is Bartlemas Fair, easily the busiest and merriest days of the summer. After days of preparation, we left the manor gay and giddy and ready for play. And today we are here. Before I left her, mother gave me ten pence for spending. I bought her a string of jet beads—3 pennies, a wooden whistle for Perkin— 2 pennies, a bone rattle for the coming babe—1 penny, and four skins of parchment for my herbal—4 pennies. In one morning, all my money gone. (p. 147)

Birdy sees a dancing bear at the fair. She is horrified to realize that its owner is going to kill it because it is so bedraggled. She promises to buy it, then has to find a way to get the money. Her bargains may help modern students understand the consumer aspects of math.

Geography and the Mississippi River

Learning about the geography of the United States is compelling when one hears firsthand accounts of travelers across the country. To learn about the Mississippi River and its vast territory, students might enjoy hearing a read-aloud from *Mississippi Solo* (1988), in which Eddie Harris recounts his solo trip in a canoe from the origin of the river to New Orleans. He recounts the high and low points of his journey, always anchoring his story in the terrain.

Rounding a bend, I see my first glimpse of the city. Buildings tall but ghost-like rise in the distant haze. Bridges hang over the river and drop their shadows into the water. And on the water, the first appearance of barges.... Minneapolis is the end of the line for barge traffic, on the Mississippi.

Or the beginning, depending on your point of view and on the barge's cargo. Oil from the gulf comes north from the gulf states and foreign oilfields to fuel and heat the north. Coal, grain, iron and steel go south. (p. 51)

Harris' writing style is relaxed but compelling. Readers feel as if they are traveling with him and learn a great deal about the traffic on the Mississippi River and the towns along it.

Conclusion

One of the principles presented in Chapter 1 comes to mind. All of the selections in this chapter were encountered while reading for pleasure. Discovering excerpts that could help teach math and geography concepts was coincidental. I never would have expected to encounter these topics while reading a mystery or science fiction. What a surprise to see equations in the middle of a historical mystery or a humorous essay. The examples in this chapter demonstrate that mathematics, geography, and literature blend beautifully.

Read-Alouds for Social Studies

4

Using facts to understand themes and concepts is an important area of study in social studies curricula. Sometimes memorization is used as an aid in this process. A major purpose of social studies is to identify, explore, and resolve value conflicts. Other social studies topics include understanding cultures and how governments work. The read-alouds selected for this chapter can contribute to all of these purposes. They include a best-selling novel, a young adult novel, a poem, and a journalistic account.

Selection 1: Value Conflict—To Memorize or Not to Memorize?

A teacher recommended *Raney* (1986), by Clyde Edgerton, to me, knowing that I would enjoy this capsule of southern life in the United States, set near where I had lived for many years. At the time I read the novel, the controversy over the importance of memorizing facts such as state capitals was rampant; even advice columnists were writing about the issue. In *Raney*, one of the characters expounds on the importance of knowing the "capols and stays," which provides a wonderful opportunity for considering this issue. When I read this passage, I marked it as a great read-aloud. In fact, the whole novel could be read aloud.

31

Raney is a Free Will Baptist from a small, rural, southern U.S. town. She marries Charles, a Methodist, who was raised in urban Atlanta. There is so much depth embedded in the humorous account of Charles's and Raney's discoveries about each other's cultures that readers will have much to ponder.

During an annual family vacation at the beach, where all family members share one cottage for a week, Uncle Nate, often inebriated, has just returned from an outing. He sits down beside Charles and initiates a conversation, but his difficulty in articulation is evident.

Activities for Social Studies

This read-aloud has great possibilities for social studies as well as language arts. One of the purposes of social studies is to identify, explore, and resolve value conflicts. This passage lends itself to resolving the value conflict of whether or not to memorize. Of what benefit is memorizing states and capitals? There may be a way to respond to both sets of values expressed here. Are other options available? Is there a better way to access important information? Does learning include memorization and, if so, to what extent? What types of learning would require memorization? Students will most likely have opinions and personal experience to argue their positions. What do their parents think and why? Have students take sides to consider the pros and cons. Such an ac-

tivity encourages lively oral discussion as well as a forum for debate.

The use of facts to understand themes and concepts is also an important area of study in social studies curricula. As an example, ask students to consider themes from geography such as location, place, relationships between people and their environments, movement, and regions. Studying state capitals could be a springboard to explore these themes. For instance, select a capital and answer the following: Where is it located? How far is it from your home? What are the latitude and longitude? What is the weather like? What are the physical and human characteristics of this place such as climate, landforms, vegetation, water, religions, languages, population, and economic activities? Given this information, why is the capital located there? Why did people move there? By reading a story, looking at a picture, or singing a song about this capital, what can a student describe about it?

Students might also use geographic knowledge for problem solving by using a map to plan a trip to their state's capital. How would one travel there—by plane, boat, car—from his or her own region? How long would the trip take? What route would one take to get there? What would there be to see or do there? How would the people be similar or different from where one lives now?

Another possible activity is to create and use a computer database into which facts about geography could be entered and then questions posed, such as,

Read-Aloud From *Raney*

Charles was over on the couch reading a "Time" magazine. Uncle Nate went over and sat down beside him.

"Wher'd you go to school, boy?"

"Atlanta."

"They teach you the stays and capols?"

"No, I don't think so."

"You don't think so? You don't think so? Wha's capol of Missesota?" He was drunker than usual.

"Missesota?"

"Minnesota."

"I don't know."

"You don't know! You don't know! St. Paul. Hell, no, they di'n teach you no capols." Uncle Nate looked around.

"Nate," says Mama, "ther'll be no cursing in this beach cottage. You have done enough damage getting drunk in front of these children. It's bad enough without you cussing in the very cottage Al Douglas has been nice enough to rent us at half price."

Uncle Nate looked at her and then turned back to Charles. "Montgomery, Alabama; Phoenix, Arizona; Little Rock, Arkansas; Sacramento, California; Denver, Colorado. Hell, I know 'em every one."

"Nate," Mama says, "now I have told you—"

"Name a stay," Uncle Nate says to Charles.

"Florida."

"Tallahassee. Ha. See? Capol T-a-l-l-a-h-a-s-s-e-e. We had to learn to spell them too. How come you din have to learn the stays and capols?"

"What good is it?" asks Charles, pushing up off the couch with his hands and slipping away.

"What good is it? Whal good is it? Why, hell, if you're traveling through Miss'ippi and somebody says 'what's the capol of this stay?' you say 'St. Paul.' You know something about the stay you're in. What good is it? What good is it? Hell, why come you learn anything?"

"Nate," says Mama.

"Well," says Charles, "I'm just thinking why not write it all down on a piece of paper, put it in your billfold, and then spend all that time learning something else. Then when somebody wants to know a capital, pull out the piece of paper and read the answer."

(continued)

"Read the answer. Read the answer. Shit, when I went to school—"

"Nate!" Mama says. "I said I was not going to have it and I mean it. If you want me to call the law you just keep it up. I'll do it. I'll do it right this very night."

Uncle Nate got quiet, almost whispering—"When I went to school you learned your lessons. You went home and learned your lessons. And when it was time to work you worked. And when it was time to go to church, you went to church. And when it was time to go to bed, you went to bed. And when it was ti—"

"Well, I'm just glad I didn't have to learn the states and capitals," said Charles.

"Well, I'm glad you learned all that," said Charles, getting up from the couch. "I think it's about time I turned in."

"I don't care if you're too good to talk to me," says Uncle Nate.

"I don't think I'm too good to talk to you."

"Oh, yes, you do." (pp. 52–53)

[From *Raney* by Clyde Edgerton. Copyright ©1986. Reprinted with permission of Algonquin Books of Chapel Hill, a division of Workman Publishing.]

Which states have the same bird or flower? Actual creation of such a database would incorporate research to find facts, decision making to determine which facts should be included, and technology to design and use the database.

A theme in social studies is understanding cultures. Although the entire novel might not be read to the social studies class, there is enough information in this passage to encourage a discussion about how people from different environments look at the same issue. Certainly from an urban to a rural location, cultures may differ. Cultural differ-ences occur even in different types of families. How do such differences alter beliefs and attitudes? Specifically, why do Charles and Uncle Nate have such differing opinions? What might they have in common? Why is Uncle Nate so upset about Charles's reaction? In what kind of environment do students think Uncle Nate was raised? How would this affect him? And what type of school must Charles have attended? How has this influenced him? Are these two characters tolerant of each other? What about their environments would contribute to the way they would get along with and communicate with each other?

Using the Social Studies Read-Aloud for Language Arts

From a language arts perspective, this passage is also very rich. Dialogue is often hard to write because the author must convey so much with the words spoken rather than with description. We have several clues to Uncle Nate's, Mama's, and Charles's characters from the dialogue. What are some of these clues? What do we know about each character from only their dialogue without any extra description? Dialogue is hard for students to write because of the punctuation required. Ask students to notice how punctuation is used to show when speakers pause, complete a thought, interrupt themselves or each other, or switch to another speaker.

What does the reader know about the characters' physical movements from this passage? These actions also reveal a great deal about the characters. This passage could be used as an act in a play. Encourage students to act out the scene, using the dialogue and the brief descriptors of movement as their script. The passage becomes a way to introduce students to drama, and to read and to learn how to write.

A possible drawback to using this passage as a read-aloud, depending on the ages of students and the community in which they live, might be the profanity Uncle Nate uses. The language the author chooses to convey Uncle Nate's character seems appropriate to the character and could stimulate a thoughtful discussion about why an author selects certain words to convey tone and mood. However, these words could be deleted without detracting from the possibilities suggested for teaching with this read-aloud.

Raney is one of the best novels I have read; I enjoyed, laughed at, and felt deeply moved by it all at the same time. Characters, plot, tone, mood, style, and theme come together in an earthy and plausible manner, and I recommend this novel to others often.

Selection 2: Considerations for Cultural Diversity

In many countries, learning to read is considered a natural part of growing up. Boys and girls start reading instruction by first grade, if not earlier. Yet, in other cultures, learning to read is not always an option. Sometimes, only the more affluent children in a culture have the opportunity to attend school; sometimes only the boys will learn to read, not the girls. Discussing opportunities to read can be a good introduction to cultural diversity for two reasons. First, because North American students take learning to read for granted, they may not realize that in other cultures learning to read is not always available. The contrast of their experience with that of children in other cultures may bring diversity into sharp relief. Second, our world is "shrinking" due to greater ease of communication. We need people in every culture who are literate and understand and appreciate all other cultures. Discussing literacy in different cultures emphasizes the importance of literacy worldwide.

The novel *Haveli* (Ha-vel´-i), by Suzanne Fisher Staples (1993), is the sequel to *Shabanu* (Sha-ban´-u), which is a Newbery Honor book. Both novels are about Shabanu, who is a member of the Cholistans, a desert culture of Pakistan. Her family is nomadic, living where they find water and raising camels on the arid land. In the first novel, 12-year-old Shabanu becomes engaged to a wealthy 52-

Read-Aloud From *Haveli*

On the morning of the first reading lesson, Shabanu squeezed her knees under the oblong table she shared with Mumtaz and the widow's children. She was enthralled with the smells of the classroom: the chalk dust, the ink on the books, the oil in the wooden floorboards.

"I am taking you to a wonderful new world," said the widow, whose name was Samiya, standing before them for the first time. "Once you've learned to read, adventures you've never even imagined will unfold. You'll visit places you never knew existed. There will be no secret you cannot unlock."

Shabanu's spirits lifted with the thought that knowing how to read could give her a new and extraordinary power over the events of her life. (page 126)

In the afternoon Samiya brought Shabanu tea. Samiya was proper and formal as she entered the room, as befitted a good servant.

But Shabanu wept when she saw the small birdlike woman. She thought of the happy days she and Mumtaz had spent with her, learning to read, learning to think, as Samiya did, that all things were possible once you had access to words in books.

"Oh, Samiya," she wept, and Samiya set down the tray without a single rattle and came swiftly on her bare feet to Shabanu's side.

"Little Begum," Samiya said, taking Shabanu's hands. She held Shabanu as she wept, and when she was finished crying she felt better.

"What else can I bring you?" asked Samiya then.

"Books!" said Shabanu. "I don't feel like reading yet, but I will soon. And a pan of coal for the heater. And more oil for the lamps. Can you do it without anyone's knowledge?" (page 257)

[From *Haveli* by Suzanne Fisher Staples. Copyright ©1993. Reprinted with permission of Alfred A. Knopf.

year-old man who already has three wives. In *Haveli*, Shabanu is 17 years old and has had a daughter, Mumtaz, who is 5 years old. Shabanu convinces her husband to take her with him to the city of Lahore to stay at the *haveli* (home) of his sister while he serves in the parliament. While in Lahore, she pleads with him to allow her to find a tutor for Mumtaz, so that their daughter might learn to read and thus have a means of livelihood in case of her father's death.

Two passages from *Haveli* demonstrate how learning to read is viewed in the Pakistani culture. The first shares Shabanu's excitement at learning to read at age 17, and the second shares how the solace of reading is all she has left after catastrophic events leave her without a family.

Connecting Social Studies, Cultural Diversity, and Language Arts

To introduce a discussion about cultural diversity, ask students to think of any events in this read aloud or in any background information provided that reflect a different way of living than in their own culture. Events such as these might be mentioned:

- Home is not a specific place, but changes according to physical needs such as where water is located. Thus some people are nomads.
- Parents decide who a daughter will marry.

- Sometimes a marriage is a means of settling a dispute or gaining land.
- Marriage is arranged when children are young, and occurs at puberty.
- Men make the major decisions, even about a woman's personal matters.
- Men can have more than one wife.
- The first wife has the most power of all a man's wives.
- A wife who bears a son has great power.
- A mentally retarded son would be chosen as a leader rather than a daughter of normal intelligence.
- Literacy is available to only a few, mostly affluent males.

Encourage students to compare and contrast Pakistani cultural beliefs to their own cultural beliefs, citing specific events to illustrate their discussion. A jot chart might be a good organizational tool for such a discussion (see the example on the following page).

Have students extend this discussion to other cultures. Focusing on literacy, guide students to think of other cultures in which learning to read might be an exclusive privilege. For instance, in *The Year of Impossible Goodbyes*, Choi (1991) relates how the North Koreans were denied books and schooling during the Japanese occupation in World War II, and then mandated to attend the communist school during the Russian occupation after the war. In *NightJohn*, Paulsen (1993)

Jot chart

Pakistani cultural belief	Event from read-aloud	Student's cultural belief	Example from own life
Learning to read is not a privilege afforded to all.	Shabanu is enthralled by chalk dust, and the power reading can give her.	Learning to read is a privilege afforded to any who want it.	I never thought about learning to read as exciting!

tells how a slave returns from freedom to teach other slaves to read.

Encourage students to write about their feelings concerning literacy after listening to and discussing this read aloud. Possible prompts might be What is the power of literacy? Why might literacy be an exclusive privilege in some cultures? How might Shabanu feel to live in North America and attend school on a daily basis? How would you feel if you were Shabanu, destined to spend years in hiding in a haveli?

Further, encourage students to write about what they have learned about Pakistani culture after the discussion. They might articulate what else they would like to learn about that culture or other cultures. Perhaps they could select a topic to research such as views of literacy, women, or marriage in another culture.

Simply telling students that cultures are diverse and providing textbook reading or lecture examples will not have the impact that sharing personal events through literature can engender. This read aloud is an effective, efficient means of introducing awareness, which can lead to insightful discussion.

Brief Selections for Social Studies

Poets Don't Always Know the History!

To demonstrate that poetry is often reflective of a historical period, but not always historically accurate, Keats's poem "On First Looking Into Chapman's Homer," (Much have I travel'd in the realms of glory) presents a good opportunity. Keats was not a historian. He writes about "stout Cortez" who stared at the Pacific Ocean from Darien's Peak in South America, but it was Vasco Nuñez de Balboa who was the first European to see the Pacific Ocean. The far-reaching effects of this re-rendering of history can be seen in P. G. Wodehouse's (1938) *The Code of the Woosters* when Bertie reminisces:

Pop Bassett, like the chap in the poem which I had to write out fifty times at school for introducing a white mouse into the English literature hour, was plainly feeling like some watcher of the skies when a new planet swims into his ken, while Aunt Dahlia and Constable Oates resembled respectively stout Cortez staring at the Pacific and all his men looking at each other with a wild surmise, silent on a peak in Darien. (p. 204)

Oral History

Nancy Rhyne takes an oral historian's approach, writing about history through the voices of people she interviews, most of whom are now advanced in age and relate their perspectives from the vantage point of age and experience. In *The Ghost of Hampton Plantation* (1997), Rhyne interviewed Sue Alston, a former slave who describes the reaction of South Carolinians to the Boston Tea Party:

> South Carolina musta been the only colony to keep the tea. Philadelphia and New York send their load back to England. And Boston? Oh, man! They dump their tea in the harbor. But South Carolina hold on to that old tea leaf and sell it to git money so they can pay for the war 'gainst England they believe was a-comin. (p. 15)

The mistress of Hampton Plantation chose to send her son to England for his education in the midst of this conflict. She paid with a shipment of rice. Alston tells how this same mistress often entertained the Swamp Fox, General Francis Marion. One time she had to hustle him out through a secret passageway just as Colonel Tarleton arrived at her door. This firsthand account from a southern perspective might liven up a study of the U.S. Revolutionary War for many 11th graders.

Writing Letters and Making a Difference in Politics

Jean Merrill's classic novel *The Push-cart Wars* (1964) demonstrates to students how one expression of opinion about a political issue can make a difference. In this novel, New York street vendors are being forced out of their favorite territories by truckers who want to park at the curbside and unload goods. Merchants want to squeeze out the pushcart vendors because they are uneasy about the competition. The vendors begin to write letters to the newspaper, and many readers respond. Eventually, a compromise is reached and the pushcart vendors are allowed to stay. "Might does not equal Right," and the voice of the people is recognized:

> This was only the beginning. Each letter to an editor that was published seemed to inspire a hundred other people to write. Buddy Wisser said that he had never received so much mail in his entire life as an editor as suddenly came to him on the subject of pushcarts. (p. 204)

After reading selected letters from the novel, ask students to read letters to the editor in their local paper and gauge the concerns of the letter writers and the possible impact the letters might have on altering a situation. Next, ask them to write letters to the editor about the pushcart vendors issue, taking either side they wish. For a more contemporary application, encourage students to think of issues that are important to them and to draft letters describing their positions.

Some students have eventually sent their letters to local newspapers. However, impress upon students the importance not only of expressing their opinions in writing, but also of writing letters that are stylistically and mechanically polished. This process takes time, a few drafts, and a consultant who will help with any needed revisions before the letter is submitted.

Conclusion

One of the principles in Chapter 1 states that read-aloud selections should encourage further reading. After reading *Raney*, I read every novel Edgerton has written. I would not have discovered the selection about literacy in Pakistan if I had not read the sequel to *Shabanu*. In "Poets Don't Always Know History!" I show how reading one selection can remind one of another selection.

One secondary student commented that he had never realized how closely related history and literature are to each other until he studied U.S. history and literature in the same year. Literature will almost always tell us something of our history and social conditions. The selections in this chapter confirm that connection.

Read-Alouds for English and Language Arts

5

This chapter contains read-alouds for several topics of study in English and language arts classes, including selections by Lois Lowry and Fred Chappel that are excellent for discussing poetry. To help students understand romanticism and realism, read aloud Gustave Flaubert's portrait of Emma. Terry Pratchett (see Chapter 3) helps liven up a spelling lesson and presents an insider's view of drama. Joyce Cary and E.B. White help readers appreciate issues of style. Lee Smith provides insights for writing.

Selection 1: What Is Poetry?

Why do so many adolescents dislike poetry? Students say they cannot understand poems; they insist that poetry must rhyme and must have capital letters as in a quatrain form—that is, poetry must conform to a specific pattern or it just isn't poetry. Other reasons, from a conversation with Leila Christenbury, past editor of the *English Journal*, are the "one right interpretation" technique and the classroom dissection of poetry followed by a test.

Scenes like the one depicted in the read-aloud concerning Anastasia Krupnik's first experience writing a poem may form negative attitudes about writing. *Anastasia Krupnik* is one of Lois Lowry's earlier novels, which appeals to elementary school readers; this excerpt, however, would most likely bring back memories to many of us of early experiences with poetry in school settings.

Anastasia is 10 years old and lives in New York City with family. She keeps a journal that contains a list of things she loves and hates. Her experiences, as recounted in each chapter, change her perspective on life and where items are placed on her list. For instance, after Mrs. Westvessel gives Anastasia's poem a grade of F, Anastasia writes Mrs. Westvessel's name under the "Things I Hate" list. But when her teacher calls to express concern and sympathy that Anastasia's grandmother has died, Anastasia changes her mind and crosses Mrs. Westvessel's name off that list.

In this novel, Anastasia is encountering many new challenges, one of which is that she is about to have a baby brother, whom she is not at all sure she wants. Another is that her grandmother lives in memories, especially of her long-deceased husband, Sam. When Anastasia visits her father's college classroom and is introduced to Wordsworth's poem, "I Wandered Lonely as a Cloud," she begins to understand and accept that "the inward eye" gives her grandmother solitude and peace.

Suggestions for Teaching Poetry

The excerpt from *Anastasia Krupnik* works well with secondary students who are studying poetry. A colleague was struck by Lowry's insight at capturing how poetry is too often perceived by students and too often taught by teachers. Lowry captures both the passionate integrity of Anastasia's views about poetry and the chillingly traditional way Mrs. Westvessel approaches the teaching of poetry.

Before the excerpt is read, share Anastasia's poem and ask questions such as, Did the author spend much time on writing this poem? (We know from reading the excerpt that she did.) How old is the author of this poem? What makes you think that? Once the excerpt is read, have students discuss their predictions with respect to information from the text. Discussion might lead students to understand more fully the process of writing poetry.

Read this excerpt aloud as an introduction to a discussion or unit on poetry. Students will begin to reflect on their opinions about poetry and how poetry has been presented to them so far in their school lives. Specifically, have students discuss the grades that each child received and Mrs. Westvessel's reasoning for the grades. This might lead students to talk openly about their views on poetry and poetry instruction.

After discussing students' opinions, read aloud the excerpt in which Anastasia shows her poem to her parents. Her father responds tactfully, complimenting his daughter on her poem but also commenting on her teacher's behavior by explaining that some people "just haven't been educated to understand poetry" (p. 17 of the same chap-

Read-Aloud From *Anastasia Krupnik*

Wednesday was the day that the members of the class were to read their own poems, aloud.

Robert Giannini stood in front of the class and read:

I have a dog whose name is Spot.

He likes to eat and drink a lot.

When I put water in his dish,

He laps it up just like a fish.

Anastasia hated Robert Giannini's poem. Also, she thought it was a lie. Robert Giannini's dog was named Sputnik; everyone in the neighborhood knew that; and Sputnik had bitten two kids during the summer and if he bit one more person the police said the Gianninis would have to get rid of him.

But Mrs. Westvessel cried, "Wonderful!" She gave Robert Giannini an A and hung his poem on the wall. Anastasia imagined that Longfellow was eyeing it with distaste.

Traci Beckwith got up from her desk, straightened her tights carefully, and read:

In autumn when the trees are brown,

I like to walk all through the town.

I like to see the birds fly south.

Some have worms, still, in their mouths.

Traci Beckwith blushed, and said, "It doesn't rhyme exactly."

"Well," said Mrs. Westvessel, in a kind voice, "your next one will be better, I'm sure." She gave Traci Beckwith a B plus, and hung the poem on the wall next to Robert's.

Anastasia had begun to feel a little funny, as if she had ginger ale inside of her knees. But it was her turn. She stood up in front of the class and read her poem. Her voice was very small, because she was nervous.

hush hush the sea-soft night is aswim

with wrinklesquirm creatures

listen(!)

to them moves smooth in the moistly dark

here in the whisperwarm wet

That was Anastasia's poem.

"Read that again, please, Anastasia, in a bigger voice," said Mrs. Westvessel.

So Anastasia took a deep breath and read her poem again. She used the same kind of voice that her father did when he read poetry to her, drawing some of the words out as long as licorice sticks, and making some others thumpingly short.

(continued)

The class laughed.

Mrs. Westvessel looked puzzled. "Let me see that, Anastasia," she said. Anastasia gave her the poem.

Mrs. Westvessel's ordinary, everyday face had about one hundred wrinkles in it. When she looked at Anastasia's poem, her forehead and nose folded up so that she had two hundred new wrinkles all of a sudden.

"Where are your capital letters, Anastasia?" asked Mrs. Westvessel.

Anastasia didn't say anything.

"Where is the rhyme?" asked Mrs. Westvessel. "It doesn't rhyme at all."

Anastasia didn't say anything.

"What kind of poem is this, Anastasia?" asked Mrs. Westvessel. "Can you explain it, please?"

Anastasia's voice had become very small again, the way voices do, sometimes. "It's a poem of sounds," she said. "It's about little things that live in tidepools, after dark, when they move around. It doesn't have sentences or capital letters because I wanted it to look on the page like small creatures moving in the dark."

"I don't know why it doesn't rhyme," she said, miserably. "It didn't seem important."

"Anastasia, weren't you listening in class when we talked about writing poems?"

Anastasia looked at the floor. "No," she whispered, finally.

Mrs. Westvessel frowned, and rubbed her juggly bosom thoughtfully. "Well," she said, at last.

"Well, Anastasia, when we talked about poetry in this class we simply were not talking about worms and snails crawling on a piece of paper. I'm afraid I will have to give you a F."

ter). He changes the "F" to "Fabulous." Ask students what criteria should be used to grade a poem, and have the students list and discuss each criterion.

Have students compare the poems of Robert, Traci, and Anastasia in terms of what their poems look like, sound like, and describe. What makes a poem bad or good? Next, have students discuss Anastasia's explanation for writing her poem. Ask students to write their own versions of each poem. To help students understand point of view, have them list their feelings and reactions as the excerpt is read or list the feelings they think Anastasia or her classmates might have had.

Invite students to examine other poets and their styles. For instance, compare the style and form of e.e. cummings to that of Carl Sandburg. Wordsworth, the poet her father introduces to Anastasia, is an excellent example.

I have students share some of their own poems with one another, but do not grade the activity. Lead a discussion of what a poem should do or say to a reader.

Activities for Integrating Poetry in Language Arts and Content Area Classrooms

English, language arts, and reading are supposed to be integrated in the secondary classroom. The following suggestions might encourage such integration.

Nilsen and Donelson (1997) encourage teachers to introduce poetry on a daily basis. Saving poetry for a unit compartmentalizes it, but sharing poetry daily shows how applicable a poem can be to one's day-to-day existence. For instance, Wordsworth's poem, "On the Banks of a Rocky Stream," can have a calming effect on a day filled with too much minutiae:

Behold an emblem of our human mind
Crowded with thoughts that need a set-
tled home,
Yet, like to eddying balls of foam,

Within this whirlpool, they each other
chase
Round and round, and neither find
An outlet nor a resting-place!
Stranger, if such disquietude be thine,
Fall on thy knees and sue for help divine.

Encourage students to bring in favorite poems to read aloud at any time. Demonstrate that poetry is often reflective of a historical period, but not always historically accurate by reading Keats's poem "On First Looking Into Chapman's Homer" (discussed in Chapter 4.) Keats was gifted at using structure as a vehicle of the historical and emotional message of the poem to convey his message. Discuss the importance of structure as a vehicle rather than structure as the entire description of poetry, as Mrs. Westvessel apparently thought.

Have students write journal entries about the read-alouds, which is a logical way to combine teacher reading, student reaction, and writing. Have students make lists such as those Anastasia kept of things to hate and love. Journal entries or lists will often inspire one to write a poem.

To integrate drama into the study of poetry, have students write and perform a one-act play or create a mime performance based on the excerpt.

To integrate art and music with the study of poetry, ask students to use color or music to represent beginning and ending emotions as an excerpt is read. Encourage students to write poetry as a way to explore many styles, forms, and topics in every content class.

Selection 2: Dreaming Poems

What is a poem? What does a poem look like? How are poems created? Who is a poet? Fred Chappell, noted author and master of the short story, encourages readers to explore these questions in his short story "Mankind Journeys Through the Forest of Symbols" in his collection *More Shapes Than One* (1991). Sheriff Balsam needs to clear a major highway of a fog so dense that motorists cannot drive through it. The fog turns out to be an unwritten poem disturbing someone's unconscious; this clouded thinking has settled on the highway. Balsam calls in the expert, Dr. Litmouse, to help find a way to dissolve the fog.

The poet turns out to be Sheriff Balsam's deputy, Bill, who sweats out his poem, which clears his head, and thus the road clears and everyone goes back to a normal life. Adolescents are bound to have fun thinking about unwritten poems fogging up unsuspecting minds and creating all kinds of havoc in a community.

Read-Aloud From *More Shapes Than One*

Dusk had come to the mountains like a sewing machine crawling over an operating table, and Dr. Litmouse and Hank and Bill and Balsam were back in the sheriff's office. Balsam sat at his desk, the telephone receiver still off the hook. Bill and Hank had resumed their corner chairs. The three lawmen were listening to the scientist's explanation.

"Basically, it's the same problem as a dream, so it's mostly out of our hands. Somebody within a fifty-mile radius is ripe to write a symbolist poem but hasn't gotten around to it yet. As soon as she or he does, then it will go away, just as the usual dream obstructions vanish when the dreamers wake." He took off his glasses and polished them with his handkerchief. His eyes looked as little and bare as shirt buttons and made the others feel queasy. They were glad when he replaced his spectacles.

"It's worse than a dream, though, because we may be dealing with a subconscious poet. It may be that this person never writes poems in the normal course of his life. If this poem originated in the mind of someone who never thinks of writing, then I'm afraid your highway detour will have to be more or less permanent." (pp. 160–161)

(continued)

The sheriff picked up a ballpoint pen and began clicking it. 'Well, let's see...There it is, and it'll go away if somebody writes it down on paper.'

"Correct." (p. 162)

"Well, what we got to do then is just get as many people as we can out there writing poems. Community effort. Maybe we'll luck out."

"How?" asked Dr. Litmouse.

He clicked his ballpoint furiously. He got a sheet of department stationery and began printing tall uncertain letters. The other three watched in suspense, breathing unevenly. When he finished, Balsam picked up the paper and held it at arm's length to read. His lips moved slightly. Then he showed them his work. "What do you think?" he asked.

THE SHERIFF'S DEPARTMENT

OF OSGOOD COUNTY

in cooperation with the

NORTH CAROLINA STATE HIGHWAY DEPARTMENT

announces

A POETRY CONTEST

$50 first prize

Send entries to SHERIFF ELMO BALSAM

OSGOOD COUNTY COURTHOUSE

EMBER FORKS, N. C. 26816

SYMBOLISM PREFERRED!!!

"I suppose it's worth a try," Dr. Litmouse said, but he sounded dubious. (pp. 162–163)

Selection 3: A Read-Aloud for Romantics and Realists

Flaubert's *Madame Bovary* illustrates a period of history, different philosophies about life, and the beauty of language. The selected passage introduces this classic and creates a "first impression." As the wife of Charles Bovary, Emma is always searching for more; she wants beauty, comfort, money, and love. She marries Charles as a means of escape; to be the wife of a country doctor seems much more appealing than her life on a country farm. However, she soon discovers that although Charles adores her, he does not share her interests. Charles is kind, gentle, dense, good-hearted, and devoted to Emma, but he will never amount to much. He is content to live in the province, without seeking out inventions and new medical procedures.

Léon, apprentice to the pharmacist Homais—a neighbor of the Bovarys—also adores Emma. Emma and Léon are avid readers and they find escape in literature. This selection foreshadows Emma and Léon's relationship. Charles's adoration of his wife and his blind acceptance of her impracticalities are apparent.

Activities for English

Ask students to notice that Emma prefers to be swept away by literature into another world. She does not seem too concerned about the present or about the feelings of others. She prefers her solitude to the company of her hus-

Read-Aloud From *Madame Bovary*

"My wife doesn't care much for it," said Charles; "she'd rather, even though she's been recommended to take exercise, stay in her room the whole time, reading."

"That's like me," remarked Léon; "what could be better, really, than an evening by the fire with a book, with the wind beating on the panes, the lamp burning?"

"I do so agree," she said, fixing on him her great black eyes open wide.

"Your head is empty," he continued, "the hours slip away. From your chair you wander through the countries of your mind, and your thoughts, threading themselves into the fiction, play about with the details or rush along the track of the plot. You melt into the characters; it seems as if your own heart is beating under their skin."

"Oh, yes, that is true," she said.

"Has it ever happened to you," Léon went on, "in a book you come across some vague idea you once had, some blurred image from deep down, something that just spells out your finest feelings?"

"I have," she answered.

"That," he said, "is why I particularly love the poets. I find verse more tender than prose, and it brings more tears to the eye."

"Though rather exhausting after a while," Emma went on; "and at the moment, you see, I adore stories that push on inexorably, frightening stories. I detest common heroes and temperate feelings, the way they are in life."

[From *Madame Bovary* by Gustave Flaubert (1857).]

Feature analysis of character qualities—romanticism vs. realism—in *Madame Bovary*

	Imaginative	Idealistic	Vivid emotions	Romantic view of death	Structured	Verifies information	Conforms to nature	Progressive
Emma	+	+	+	+	−	−	−	−
Homais	−	−	−	−	+	+	+	+
Léon	+	+ at first	+	?	+ at end	+ at end	?	+ at end
Charles	−	−	−	+ at end	+	−	+ as led	−

band or child. She does not like things the way they are in life. Ask what students think of this view. What does the reader know about Emma from just this passage? Of Léon?

Direct students to consider several themes in *Madame Bovary*. The universality of these questions would most likely appeal to teenagers: When a situation seems untenable, what can one do? What choices do we have? Is it OK to hurt others if we ourselves have a chance to be happy? Is it OK to become successful at the expense of others? What is most important in life: money, happiness, comfortable surroundings, or progress? Is progress inevitable? Is change always a desirable thing? As students read, they may think about their own responses as well as those of the characters.

Flaubert wrote in an age when romanticism was waning and realism was taking hold. To help English students understand Flaubert's characters as they symbolize traits of romanticism and realism, use the feature analysis chart shown above. Although the chart provides suggested responses, students may have different opinions. Encourage them to express opinions based on contextual evidence, which will enhance oral communication skills.

Starting with the read-aloud passage, ask students what indications of romantic and realistic qualities can be found? Students should read the entire novel in order to consider features of other characters. Encourage students to find character actions in this novel that depict features of romanticism and realism.

Ask students, What do the names of characters imply? They may call Charles Bovary the "bovine," which is most likely what Flaubert had in mind. Emma's name is very close to the French word *femme*, meaning woman. Homais's name is very close to the French word *homme*, meaning man. Both Emma and Homais desire change; both possess energy and vision; however, their solutions are very different, and neither one has settled on a satisfying life.

Activities for Language Arts

Use this read-aloud to inspire discussion about the reasons we read. Ask students if they read to be carried away into the story. Do they read as Léon does: to "wander through the countries of your mind, and your thoughts, threading [themselves] into the fiction, play about with the details or rush along the track of the plot? You melt into the characters; it seems as if your own heart is beating under their skin." Do they want to be frightened or live in another world? Ask what other reasons they read. Ask what these preferences indicate about their personalities. Discuss how reading tastes and choices change with our moods.

Discuss the differences between poetry and prose. Léon prefers poetry because it is more tender and emotional. Do students agree? Have them find examples to support their opinions.

After completing the features analysis chart of the romantic and realistic characteristics of the characters in *Madame Bovary*, have students write a comparative essay. This assignment combines writing with content knowledge. Or have students select a question from those mentioned and write an essay expressing their own opinion, that of at least two of the novel's characters, and that of Flaubert.

This selection demonstrates several components of a novel: theme, characters, plot, and irony. Setting is also richly developed and connects this novel to a historical study of the era. Industrial-ism influenced the realistic view, and while Charles Bovary was content to maintain the old ways, others were marching on. Homais read the newspapers, wanted the newest transportation, and wanted to try experiments. Have students select a character in this novel who best illustrates a lesson about progress. Using examples from the novel, have students present their arguments orally.

Flaubert writes from the woman's point of view in this novel. By employing Emma's voice, he depicts the role of the 18th-century woman. Does he think that women are repressed? Is he an early feminist? A colleague once compared Emma to Frankenstein's monster. *Frankenstein* (1831) by Mary Shelley is written from the male monster's point of view. Both Emma and the monster are bound by the limitations placed on them. Emma, encouraged to be idealistic and ambitious, was limited by her education; Dr. Frankenstein's monster created with a damaged brain, was limited. Have students choose a favorite character from another novel and compare the character to one in *Madame Bovary*.

Flaubert has taken a mundane plot line and created a great story. Your challenge is to enable teenagers to appreciate this novel. Starting with a read-aloud in which an ordinary conversation about an activity most of us engage in regularly—reading—and moving to a discussion of universal themes is an effective way to hook young readers.

Brief Selections for English and Language Arts

The Importance of Correct Spelling

Terry Pratchett is a popular author of fantasy and humor in Great Britain. His books have become increasingly popular in the United States as well. *Witches Abroad* (1991) provides an excellent read-aloud about the importance of spelling and about homophones.

About Drama

Pratchett's *Wyrd Sisters* (1988) provides a wonderful introduction to the-

ater for language arts classes. In this novel, the witches hide the crown prince from an evil duke who has usurped the throne; they place the prince with a company of actors. TomJohn becomes one of the best actors in the troupe. Ironically, his company is commissioned by the duke to stage a play in which the witches are portrayed as evil hags. Ask students, Why do we enjoy plays? What happens when we watch a play?

Style and Readability

In his essay, "The Calculating Machine," E.B. White writes about his irri-

---

Read-Aloud From *Witches Abroad*

Local people called it the Bear Mountain. This was because it was a bare mountain, not because it had a lot of bears on it. This caused a certain amount of profitable confusion, though; people often strode into the nearest village with heavy duty crossbows, traps and nets and called haughtily for native guides to lead them to the bears. Since everyone locally was making quite a good living out of this, what with the sale of guide books, maps of bear caves, ornamental cuckoo-clocks with bears on them, bear walking-sticks and cakes baked in the shape of a bear, somehow no one had time to go and correct the spelling.*

*Bad spelling can be lethal. For example, the greedy seriph of Al-Ybi was once cursed by a badly-educated deity and for some days everything he touched turned to Glod, which happened to be the name of a small dwarf from a mountain community hundreds of miles away who found himself magically dragged to the kingdom and relentlessly duplicated. Some two thousand Glods later the spell wore off. These days, the people of Al-Ybi are renowned for being unusually short and bad-tempered. (pp. 11–12).

[From *Witches Abroad*. Copyright ©1991 by Terry & Lyn Pratchett. London: Victor Gollancy Ltd. Reprinted with permission of Colin Smythe.]

Read-Aloud From *Wyrd Sisters*

Granny subsided into unaccustomed, troubled silence, and tried to listen to the prologue. The theatre worried her. It had a magic of its own, one that didn't belong to her, one that wasn't in her control. It changed the world, and said things were otherwise than they were. And it was worse than that. It was magic that didn't belong to magical people. It was commanded by ordinary people, who didn't know the rules. They altered the world because it sounded better. (p. 265)

tation upon receiving a pocket calculating device that will "help" authors write more clearly. This "Reading-Ease-Calculator" is based on a readability formula that measures word and sentence length. White is not very impressed.

The poor fellow! His leading essay, the one on the front cover, tested Very Hard.

White goes on to say,

There is, of course, no such thing as reading ease of written matter. There is ease with which matter can be read, but that is a condition of the reader, not of the matter. Thus the inventors and distributors of this calculator get off to a poor start, with a Very Hard instruction book and a slovenly phrase. Already they have one foot caught in the brier patch of English usage....

Communication by the written word is a subtler (and more beautiful) thing than Dr. Flesch and General Motors imagine. There is no average reader, and to reach down toward this mythical character is to deny that each of us is on the way up, is ascending. (pp. 165–166)

[From *The Second Tree From the Corner* by E.B. White (1951). Harper & Row.]

This essay stimulates discussion of what makes good writing: Is it the words used? Is it the intricacy of the sentences? Is it the way sentences are arranged? Can good writing be measured and assigned a reading level?

Style and Choice of Tense

In his prefatory essay about *Mr. Johnson*, Cary (1952) writes,

As for the style of the book, critics complained of the present tense. And when I answered that it was chosen because Johnson lives in the present, from hour to hour, they found this reason naïve and superficial. (p. 7)

For I came to understand something in that moment, Joli, which I had never un-derstood in all of these years.

The letters didn't mean anything.

Not to the dead girl Silvaney, of course—nor to me.

It was the writing of them that signified. (p. 313)

[From *Fair and Tender Ladies* by Lee Smith. Copyright ©1988. G.P. Putnam's Sons.]

What is style? What factors create a good style of writing? What books do students prefer? Does style influence their choices? Is using the present tense acceptable to them? What role should critics play in judging an author's style? Cary points out that,

> For a reader (who may have as much critical acumen as you please, but is not reading in order to criticize), the whole work is a single continuous experience. He does not distinguish style from action or character. (p. 8)

Cary stirs up a controversy and provides a wonderful opportunity for students to discuss what makes good writing.

Reasons for Writing

In *Fair and Tender Ladies*, Lee Smith helps students understand the writing process through letters by a girl growing up in Appalachia. At the end of the novel, the girl has grown old and has retired to a cabin in the mountains. Her daugh-ter is quite concerned about her and her odd habits. Ivy tries to explain why she has just burned all of her old letters.

We write first and foremost for our-selves. We write to learn about ourselves. Often no one else will ever read what we write. Ivy learned about herself as she wrote her letters. The author shows us through Ivy's letters how writing can help us grow.

This selection helps explain to stu dents the different kinds of writing they might do. To learn, one jots notes or writes in a journal as Ivy does—or as Annie Dillard does (see Chapter 2). Eventually, these notes may become published writing, then the writing must be polished. The stylistic issues that White (1951) and Cary (1952) discuss become important.

Conclusion

The variety of genres in this chapter help explain why, in Chapter 1, I suggest-ed reading widely from many genres of literature. A children's novel and a short story written for adults illustrate both the simplicity and complexities of poetry. Both illustrate important insights about poetry in a humorous manner. Secondary students sometimes dismiss classics such as *Madame Bovary* because they think the content is not relevant to them. However, classics are a part of the English teacher's curriculum and skillful teachers can make connections using carefully selected excerpts and guided discussion. Humor and fantasy can enliven the study of orthography, and essays allow students to see the author's point of view and reactions to criticism. Letters can reveal a life story: Variety is the spice of life.

Read-Alouds for Music, Art, and Health/ Physical Education

6

The read aloud selections in this chapter will provide some new ways to promote reading to learn in these content areas. The selections in this chapter are from a children's book, science fiction, young adult fiction, and an essay.

Selection 1: An Operatic Read-Aloud for Music and Art

Jealousy! Loyalty! Invasion! Captivity! Trickery! Punishment! Death! These elements of successful novels are present in the picture book rendition of the operatic story, *Aida*, as retold by opera diva Leontyne Price. Many students find opera difficult to understand and enjoy because they are unaware of an underlying story. By introducing *Aida* through a read-aloud, students will know the story, and their "comfort level" with opera will rise. The connection Price makes between herself and her character in the epilogue also encourages an understanding of the drama of opera.

This picture book, based on the opera composed by Giuseppe Verdi in the latter part of the 19th century, is appropriate for introducing adolescent and adult readers to opera.

Read-Aloud From *Aida*

Aida as a heroine—and Aida as an opera—has been meaningful, poignant, and personal for me. In many ways, I believe Aida is a portrait of my inner self.

She was my best friend operatically and was a natural for me because my skin was my costume. This fact was a positive and strong feeling and allowed me a freedom of expression, of movement, and of interpretation that other operatic heroines I performed did not. I always felt, while performing Aida, that I was expressing all of myself—as an American, as a woman, and as a human being. (Epilogue)

[From *Aida* by Leontyne Price. Illustrated by Leo and Diane Dillon. Copyright ©1998. Gulliver Books, Harcourt Brace.]

Aida has been popular for more than a century because its appealing love story is accompanied by music, which usually is recognized instantly even by listeners who have little knowledge of opera. *Aida* is most likely based on an actual event in history; Verdi relied on a story by Camille du Locie, who most likely borrowed his plot from Françoise Auguste Ferdinand Mariette. The original story was "brought to light during an archeological excavation in Egypt" (End Notes, *Aida*).

In the story, war is raging between Egypt and Ethiopia. In an Egyptian raid, Aida is captured and taken to Memphis where she is enslaved to the Egyptian princess, Amneris. Aida does not reveal her own identity as princess of Ethiopia, lest she cause greater devastation to her people. She does confide in Radames, a captain in the Egyptian army, with whom she has fallen in love. It is his dream to become leader of the Egyptian army, win a battle with Ethiopia, marry Aida, and then restore her to her rightful place as Queen of Ethiopia. Eventually, Radames is condemned to death in a sealed vault unless he agrees to wed Amneris and never again see Aida. Thinking that at least Aida is safe, Radames descends to his death in the vault. Suddenly, he hears Aida's voice and discovers that she has hidden herself in the airless vault where they embrace and die peacefully together.

Activities for Music

The richness of the story is enhanced by the elaborate and picturesque strains composed by Verdi. To introduce the opera, first play the overture for approximately 2 minutes prior to reading the book. Have students brainstorm moods and types of events that might occur in the story from this brief musical encounter. Turn the pages and note the illustrations as the music is heard. Next, have students enjoy the full overture, following along and speculating what events or feelings the music might be depicting such as the capture of Aida, the triumphal return of Radames, and the sealing of the vault. The musical contrast of moods is evident and should lead to interest in and discussion about how the music is used to portray the events of the story. For a third activity, play the entire opera with Italian lyrics while students imagine the story taking place.

Three celebrated complete performances of *Aida* are available on video. The most recently recorded version (1989) features Aprile Millo as Aida and Placido Domingo as Radames. A 1988 video features Maria Chiara as Aida and Luciano Pavarotti as Radames. The 1962 video may be of particular interest because Leontyne Price is Aida with Jon Vickers as Radames. If the videos are available, have groups of students view one of the three productions. Because there are differences, each group could present the same scene as interpreted by the different versions. For instance, have each group play for the other groups the scene in which King Amonasro hides to surprise Aida while she waits for Radames. Have students compare the singers' interpretations, demeanors, voice qualities, intensity, costumes, orchestral renditions, and set design.

Activities for Art

Just as the music and lyrics of *Aida* are rich in their tone and intensity, the illustrations in this picture book edition by the Caldecott Medal Award winning artists, Leo and Diane Dillon, are elaborate tapestries in royal, bold colors. Each borderd illustration contains extreme detail. Even the title and end pages deserve scrutiny. If students are able to view one or more of the videos, have them compare the multidimensional set, cast, and costume interpretations with the one-dimensional book illustrations in terms of detail, design, color, elaboration, and techniques used. Have students draw ideas from each production and decide specifically how they would produce that act.

Because the Dillons have illustrated many books with an African or African American theme, a media center scavenger hunt for their books and videos would allow students to locate many of their illustrations. The hunt would encourage students to use their library search skills and motivate them visually to examine, compare, and discuss the discovered works for illustrative style, media used, the appropriateness of illustrations for a given story, and the degree to which the illustrations enhance or detract from the text. Recommended titles illustrated by the Dillons include *Ashanti to Zulu: African Traditions* (1976); *Why Mosquitoes Buzz in People's Ears: A West African Tale* (1992); and *Many Thousand Gone: African Americans From Slavery to Freedom* (1995).

Because Africa is a large continent, art will differ among the countries. Where is Ethiopia? Where is Egypt? Would their art forms likely be similar at similar periods of history? Have students tell about styles and forms of art from the Dillons' illustrations.

Connecting Music, Art and Language Arts

Based on an oral overview to page 5 of the story, encourage students to predict what might have occurred prior to the time Radames is appointed commander of the Egyptian army. Next, have them predict what events might follow, which will result in cause and effect speculation. Ask students either to read or listen to the whole story to prove or disprove their predictions. Eighth-grade students made the following predictions based on the selected excerpt:

Cause Predictions	Effect Predictions
Aida was made a slave.	Radames chose Aida.
Aida was from the enemy country.	Amneris will cause trouble.
Aida might have been afraid.	Amneris and Aida will fight.
They saw each other secretly before.	Radames gets to be the leader.
Egypt and Ethiopia are at war.	The Ethiopians will attack Egypt.
Radames helped capture Aida.	Egyptians will attack Ethiopia.

Draw open-ended lines at the end of the initial brainstormed predictions so reflective students may note additional possibilities or add actual causes and effects based on the excerpt when the entire book is read. Guide students to eliminate earlier inappropriate predictions. This will help students to evaluate their initial predictions and to consider what they learned by reviewing the complete text.

Price uses descriptive language to create visual images for her readers. Examples include "fair as the sunrise and gentle as starlight touching a flower" (p. 1); "her fury was interrupted by the trumpets heralding" (p. 7); "her heart was torn" (p. 9); and "dancing girls threw rose petals to form a welcoming carpet" (p. 13). Encourage students to find additional examples in the text and discuss the specific images the language produces as they visualize what is being described. In turn, have them apply this descriptive style to their own writing.

The characters in *Aida* are clearly defined by explicit traits. A character trait structured overview (see page 59) for a character of choice can be developed to give plot support for a given character's traits. The graphic organizer offers one structure for students to analyze many character's traits. This organizer can be used as a prewriting reference to help students develop one or more paragraphs describing and supporting the traits of a selected character.

Character trait structured overview—Amneris

Traits		
Vain	Jealous	Remorseful

Events supporting traits		
Pleased with reflection in mirror	Furious when Radames showed interest in Aida	Sorry she didn't stop guards when they took Radames away
Thought Radames should be taken by her beauty	Tricked Aida to think Radames was dead	Prayed on Radames's grave
	Spied on Radames and called him a traitor	Asked gods for forgiveness
	Made Radames a prisoner when he chose Aida	

Activities for Drama and Writing

Aida lends itself naturally to dramatic interpretation, which some students may appreciate through viewing one or more of the videos suggested previously. Divide the class into groups of at least five students, with each student assuming one of the following character roles: Aida, Radames, Amneris, Amonasro, and the Pharaoh. If there are additional students, other roles such as the High Priest might be included, or several students might play one or more characters. Have each group plan and present either an improvised version of the story or a more rehearsed dramatization. Have students discuss and compare their various interpretations. By videotaping, the playbacks can be used for comparison.

Aida also inspires creative writing. Story modifications may be entertained and brainstormed. After all, Verdi wrote his opera based on a historical event. A possible prewriting discussion could include the following questions:

1. What if Amneris had fallen in love with an Ethiopian male captive?

2. What if Radames did not return from his attack on Ethiopia and was imprisoned there?

3. What if Radames had defected and escaped with Aida?

4. What if Aida had not been able to sneak into the vault undetected?

After discussion, encourage students in groups or individually to develop their own versions of this classic by modifying story elements and events or by adding a next chapter or sequel.

The book *100 Great Operas and Their Stories* (1960) by Henry Simon provides act-by-act synopses of operas, including

Aida. Have students compare the synopses of *Aida* with the Price story to help articulate differences between narrative and exposition. Have students consider why each style of writing is suitable to a particular format, as well as which they would prefer and why. A possible independent writing assignment might be to select another opera and write both a synopsis and a storybook for it.

Students expressing interest in knowing more about opera after experiencing this picture book should be encouraged to read, research, and view additional resources like the video *The Life of Verdi* (1983)or unique books about the opera in general, such as *Great Operatic Disasters* (1979)and *Who's Afraid of Opera?* (1994). A positive exposure through this picture book will introduce students to opera in such an inviting way that they will choose to explore this artistic form further.

Selection 2: Music as Communication

Although I have very little musical talent, I enjoy listening to music. In my leisure reading, I have discovered several passages in which music is featured, making me realize that music can have a major impact on one's life.

This read-aloud from Sheri Tepper's (1987) science-fiction novel *After Long Silence* is set on a planet where huge crystalline structures dominate the landscape. The humans who have colonized this world believe themselves to be its only prescient life form. The planet seems ideal for permanent settlement, except that the crystal structures shatter whenever anyone tries to pass between them, wounding or killing the unwary traveler. Naturally, this circumstance limits mobility and causes great difficulty in trade and communication. Some individuals, however, have a talent for navigating the caverns of crystal by singing their way through them; these "Tripsingers" are the only ones who can travel in relative safety. The "Presences," as named by the Tripsingers, remain stable when music is sung, but only if the music conforms to specific requirements. Consequently, the Tripsingers are constantly exploring and experimenting for the musical combinations that work. Sometimes lives are lost during the trials. One solution would be to destroy all of the crystalline structures, which a particularly powerful and evil group is plotting to do. However, the musicians know intuitively that these structures are prescient. The only way they can prove this is to establish a means of communication.

Activities for Communicating With Music

In addition to being good science fiction, *After Long Silence* is a wonderful exploration of music as communication. (Unfortunately, this book is out of print, but check libraries or used bookstores.)

The Presences may be similar to whales, who constantly sing in order to

Read-Aloud From *After Long Silence*

Then they tried rushing past the Jam...the Jam...the Presences, and somebody tried to sing them through and couldn't and everybody got squashed and ripped apart and...well, you know. It was bloody and awful. (page 5)

A scant twenty miles away the monstrous hulk of the Enigma quivered darkly against the Old Moon, a great, split pillar guarding the wall between the interior and the southern coast. Was the new score really a password past the Presence? Or would it be just one more failed attempt, ending in blood and death? The Enigma offered no comment, simply went on quivering, visibly occulting the stars at its edge in a constant shimmer of motion.

He turned to the west in a wide arc, ticking off the Presences along the horizon. Enigma, Sky Hammer, Amber Axe, Deadly Dozen, Cloud Gatherer, Black Tower, the Far Watchlings, then the western escarpment of crowded and mostly unnamed Presences. A little south of west were the Twin Watchers. The Watcher score was one of the first Passwords he had ever learned—a fairly simple piece of singing, with phonemes that were easy to get one's tongue around. "Arndaff duh-roomavah," he chanted softly, "sindir dassalam awoh" wondering as he occasionally did if there was really any meaning in the sounds. Official doctrine taught there was not, that the sounds, when properly sung and backed up with appropriate orchestration, merely damped the vibration in the crystalline Presences, thus allowing caravans to get through. (p. 9)

[From *After Long Silence* by Sheri Tepper. Copyright ©1987. Reprinted with permission of Bantam Books.]

communicate with each other. Music can provide consonance or soothe the soul, as it does literally in this novel. But dissonance makes listeners uncomfortable, as is often its purpose. Through the ages, dissonance has provided variety in music, enabling listeners to feel emotions more fully, to prickle the senses, and to cause listeners to pay attention. The siren of an ambulance, for instance, produces discordant sound to make motorists pay attention and yield the right of way.

The Tripsingers do not discover, until late in the novel, that the Presences can actually communicate with humans; whereas consonance keeps them calm and asleep, dissonance wakes them up. However, once the Presences have been alerted, they expect to communicate and are displeased when they are disturbed for no reason. Ask students what kind of music would most likely soothe the Presences. Would it encourage communication? Would it be jazz, new age, classical, rock? Would it be soft or loud? Would it be fast or slow?

Connecting Musical Communication and Language Arts

Ask students to note how oral language can convey expression that the written message cannot. When one says "Oh, sure," the expression connotes agreement or sarcasm, depending on the tone of voice. Ask students how one would write a dialogue to convey such nuances: short, forceful words, for staccato effect. When would longer, sibilant words work best? When reading aloud, should one murmur or shout, read quickly or slowly?

Selection 4: The Appeal of Music

The read-aloud from *A Solitary Blue* (1983), a young adult novel by Cynthia Voigt, explores a boy's struggle to accept that his mother is a free spirit who has little regard for home and family. She abandoned Jeff when he was very young, and he has been reared by his absent-minded, reserved father. When Jeff visits his mother, Melody, for the first time, he is captivated by everything she does, including her amateurish guitar playing. Upon returning home, he expresses interest in the guitar, so his father and Brother Thomas take him to listen to a string concert. Jeff tries very hard not to like the music because he is afraid that appreciating this wonderful music will mean he has betrayed his mother. Yet Jeff cannot resist the music's appeal.

Over time, Jeff and his father struggle with their relationship. Theirs is a quiet undemonstrative relationship, yet they come to respect, understand, and love each other. When his mother shows up one day hoping to take Jeff away with her, he knows that he does not want to go. He has grown beyond what she can offer him.

A major theme in this novel is the complexity of relationships, particularly between parents and adolescents. Melody cannot offer Jeff enough, just as she cannot play the guitar very well. On the other hand, because he plays the guitar expertly, Julian Bream creates harmony (see page 63) In music, melody is the basic tune, while harmony is the group of notes that enhances the tune and makes it interesting. Jeff has learned to love his mother, but he needs more in his life than she can offer.

Activities for the Appeal of Music

Another theme evident in this excerpt is the "pull" of music, the way in which it can evoke mood and emotion. When I read the line "He felt the music enter his body and flow along his blood," I was

Read-Aloud From *A Solitary Blue*

The concert surprised Jeff, caught him unaware. It was given at the Peabody Institute, in a narrow auditorium room that was crowded with people. Julian Bream came onto the stage carrying his own chair to sit on, and the audience clapped for just a little bit, then stopped, rustling into an eager silence. Jeff couldn't see the musician clearly, just a figure on a chair on the stage, holding what looked like a misshapen guitar. But when he started to play and the music filled the air of the room, winding and weaving until it lay over Jeff like a net, Jeff almost forgot to breathe. It was like guitar music, the plucking on strings, the tones reverberated out from the belly of the instrument, the one hand on the neck, the other on the strings; but it rang like church bells, quiet church bells. Melodic lines, chords, harmonies—how the almost motionless figure could make such complicated music Jeff did not know. He felt the music enter his body and flow along with his blood.

Some of the pieces were slow, some in quicker rhythm, some were one simple clear line and others were dense progressions of chords. For a long time Jeff gave himself over to the music.

Until he realized what he was doing and then he tried to stop. He resisted the notes as they called out to him, because he could hear how weak and thin Melody's songs were in comparison to this man's mastery. The concert was wonderful, but he wouldn't let it capture him. When he found himself sitting forward in his seat, he made himself lean back. He forced his eyes to wander over the rest of the audience rather than stay riveted to the figure on the stage. If he was Melody's knight, he could admit no imperfection in his service to her, no disloyalty.

"How'd you like it?" Brother Thomas asked him as they made their slow way out of the auditorium. "Isn't he something?"

Jeff nodded in agreement and added, in honesty, "I've never heard anything like it. Thank you." Music with song was one of his links to Melody, and nothing would come before that; but he couldn't deny the truth, so he said, "It was wonderful."
(pp. 54–55)

[From *A Solitary Blue* by Cynthia Voigt. Copyright ©1983. Reprinted with permission of Atheneum Books for Young Readers, an imprint of Simon & Schuster Children's Publishing Division.]

reminded of the story behind Ken Burns's selection of "Ashoken Farewell" as background music for his series *The Civil War*. "Ashoken Farewell"was written by Jay Ungar to express his sorrow at the end of his summer music workshops, when participants had to depart. Burns had heard the piece played and knew it would be just right to convey the sadness underlying his documentary.

Students might be interested in this story, too, as an example of how music can remind listeners of situations outside of the current scene. Tchaikovsky's *1812 Overture*, for instance, evokes emotions beyond that period of history. Encourage students to think of music they have heard that pulls at them and reminds them of something special.

Connecting the Appeal of Music to Language Arts

Writing opportunities would connect music and language arts. Music students must use words to describe and analyze a piece. A journal entry in which students describe either a live concert attended or one viewed on television could then lead to a class discussion: What was the scene like before the concert? How did you feel during the concert? How would you describe what went on? Did you want to like this music; did you try to resist it? Why? Play a recording, perhaps of "Ashoken Farewell,"and encourage students to jot down the words that come to mind as they listen.

When I read *Solitary Blue* aloud, students wanted to know who Melody was and why Jeff would fight so hard against enjoying the music. Their reactions may typify those of other listeners and show how this read-aloud passage could introduce a book talk, encourage the reading of this book, or lead to a good discussion about music and communication.

Selection 4: A True Story for Physical Education

Paul Harvey, noted for his radio program in which he tells"the rest of the story,"presented a true story about two football coaches from Paul Aurandt's *Destiny* (1983). Percy Haughton of Harvard University (Massachusetts) had a winning record and was a no-nonsense coach. Glenn (Pop) Warner of Carlisle, Pennsylvania, became the country's best known coach during his tenure there. Pop was very creative. He devised a strategy to baffle the opposing team. Into each player's jersey he added padding that looked like a football to confuse the opposing players about who really had the ball. This tactic had helped his team defeat Syracuse, and now was hoped to work against Harvard.

After some thought, Coach Haughton found a solution: When Warner went to select a football to start the game, he found that every football in the bag was dyed crimson, the color of Harvard's jerseys.

Read-Aloud From *Destiny*

To Harvard's Coach Haughton, such trickery was unsportsmanlike. "Whiff-Whaff," he called it. To ensure a victory, Pop Warner had resorted to "whiff-whaff."

The night before the big Harvard-Carlisle contest Haughton actually approached Pop, asking whether he planned to use the trick jerseys for the next day's game. Warner smiled. "Nothing in the rules says we can't," Pop replied, and Haughton turned away. It seemed that Harvard had been defeated even before the first play. (p. 17)

[From *Destiny* by Paul Aurandt. Copyright ©1983. Bantam Books/William Morrow.]

This excerpt could launch a discussion of sportsmanship: Was Pop Warner playing fair? Could his "whiff-whaff" work today? Was Coach Haughton's solution fair? What is a good definition of sportsmanship? What behaviors demonstrate sportsmanship? Ask students for other solutions to the dilemma Coach Haughton faced.

Many high school coaches encourage their students to play with the mind as well as the body. Does this incident fit that advice? Ask the students if they have heard of or read about any similar incidents in sports. Before reading to the end, have students predict the rest of the story. Who won this game? (Harvard won, 17 to 0.)

Conclusion

One way to discover good read-alouds is to talk with other teachers. After I read *A Solitary Blue* and *After Long Silence*, I talked to a professor of music education. As a result, I developed a deeper appreciation and better sense of music. I try to convey in this chapter what I learned from her explanations. The selections in this chapter may guide many students to "the rest of the story."

List of Musical Resources for Verdi

Castellani, R. (1983) *The Life of Verdi*. [video] London: RAI-Antenne 2-Bavaria, BBC-SVT2-TSS Co. Production.

Verdi, G. (1962). *Aida*. New York: London Records; distributed by PolyGram [video].

Verdi, G. (1986). *Aida* [video]. Milan, Italy: RM Arts. Ente Autonomo Teatro all Scala and Radiotelvisione Italiana.

Verdi, G. (1989). *Aida* [video]. Hamburg, Germany: Deutsche Grammophon; distributed by PolyGram, New York.

Verdi, G. (1994). *Aida* [CD and LD]. New York: Sony Classical.

Verdi, G. (1995). *Aida*. Munich, Germany: HNH International; distributed by MVD Music and Video.

Verdi, G. (1996). *Aida*. [CD and libretto]. Los Angeles: Black Dog; Leventhal, and EMI Records.

7

Read-Alouds for Second Language Learners

Learning a second language depends on several conditions. For some learners, a second language comes quite easily, but for others the learning is more challenging. Learning a second language takes time. Many factors must be considered in planning instruction. This chapter reveals some of the basic issues about language acquisition such as amount of exposure to the second language, individual characteristics of learners, aptitude for language, cognitive style, personality, overload of concepts, motivation, and cultural considerations. Three literature selections show how protagonists learn a second language. The fourth selection provides a way to show learners that meaning can be conveyed very differently from language to language, depending on the translator.

Selection 1: Becoming a Language Master

The Count of Monte Cristo, Edmund Dantès, was a language master. How did he develop such facility? The selected excerpts help demonstrate some principles of learning second, third, and even fourth languages. Reading choices are made in surprising ways, as I stated in Chapter 1. I was inspired to read *The Count of Monte Cristo* by Alexandre Dumas after viewing the movie *Sleepers*.

In the movie, four preadolescent boys steal hot dogs from a New York City vendor. As the vendor chases three of the boys, the fourth pushes the vendor's cart to a new location. Unfortunately, the prank goes awry when the cart crashes down the steps of a subway station and into an innocent commuter. The boys are sentenced to a correctional institute, where they are submitted to brutal treatment from older prisoners and guards. The prison school offers a respite; the teacher assigns *The Count of Monte Cristo*. In the character Dantès, the boys see a kindred spirit—here is another prisoner who ultimately escapes his gruesome surroundings and gets revenge on those who have made his life so miserable.

Edmund Dantès as a young man seems to have a promising career as a ship captain, but jealous peers contrive to send him to prison for carrying a message from Napoleon. Although Dantès is innocent of any political motivation, he is a victim of his own good intentions in trying to carry out a deathbed wish of his captain; he promised to deliver a letter to someone in Paris. Dantès is arrested for this deed. The villains of this story, who betray Dantès, become successful at his expense.

Dantès is thrown into a dungeon, where he languishes. Eventually, the Abbé Busoni, located in another cell in the dungeon, tunnels through to Dantès's cell and they become friends. The abbé teaches Dantès philosophy and several languages. He also shares with Dantès the location of a secret treasure, which he wills to Dantès. Dantès contrives an elaborate escape from prison by hiding in the dead abbé's body bag, which is tossed into the sea. He locates the treasure on the rock island of Monte Cristo, becomes extraordinarily wealthy, takes the title of Count, and proceeds to Paris to exact revenge on his enemies in the guise of the Count of Monte Cristo.

Activities for Second Language Learners

Dantès is able to accomplish his vendetta because he has become rich and because he speaks so many languages like a native which enables him to gain the trust of his victims. How does one learn to speak another language with such facility? How could Dantès pull this off so well that his close friends all think he is a native of their own countries?

Introduce students to some basic issues in language acquisition: phonemic and syntactic awareness, type of exposure to language, time, individual characteristics of learners, aptitude for language, cognitive style of learners, personality of learners, and motivation. How native-sounding one becomes depends greatly on these issues.

The type of exposure a learner experiences will make a difference in what is learned and how long that learning takes. Some theorists present two basic ways in which a second language can be learned; both are important. For in-

Read-Aloud From *The Count of Monte Cristo*

Dantès possessed a prodigious memory, combined with an astonishing quickness and readiness of conception. The mathematical turn of his mind rendered him apt at all kinds of calculation, while his naturally poetical feelings threw a light and pleasing veil over the dry reality of arithmetical computation or the rigid severity of lines. He already knew Italian, and had also picked up a little of the Romaic dialect, during his different voyages to the East; and by the aid of these two languages he easily comprehended the construction of all the others, so that at the end of six months he began to speak Spanish, English, and German. (p. 145)

"My kingdom is bounded only by the world, for I am neither an Italian, nor a Frenchman, nor a Hindoo, nor an American, nor a Spaniard. I am a cosmopolitan. No country can say it saw my birth. God alone knows what country will see me die. I adopt all customs, speak all languages. You believe me to be a Frenchman, for I speak French with the same facility and purity as yourself. Well, Ali, my Nubian, believes me to be an Arab; Bertuccio, my steward, takes me for Roman; Haydée, my slave, thinks me a Greek." (p. 495)

"You know, sir, I do not speak French?"
"I know you do not like to converse in our language," replied the envoy.
"But you may use it," replied Lord Wilmore; "I understand it."
"And I," replied the visitor, changing his idiom, "know enough of English to keep up the conversation. Do not put yourself to the slightest inconvenience."
"Heighho!" said Lord Wilmore, with that tone which is only known to natives of Great Britain." (p. 691)

[From *The Count of Monte Cristo* by Alexandre Dumas (1852). Oxford University Press edition.]

stance, Dantès needed formal, cognitive skills to read and write documents in many languages. He needed informal skills to communicate informally at the many parties he attended. He did so well with both that people assumed he was a native speaker of whatever language he was speaking.

Some people naturally learn more quickly than others do. Some have greater verbal skills. Aptitude for learning will play a part in second language acquisition. A learner's cognitive style also will help or hinder the learning process. People who tend to learn holistically may grasp the pitch, tone, and expressions of a new language quickly, whereas people who learn analytically may see the grammatical details more easily. Personality also plays a role. Those who are more introverted may be quieter and listen carefully to users of the second language, which allows them to hear and understand the new language. Those who are more extroverted may seek opportunities to try out the new language. Using the excerpt as a base for discussion, along with the plot summary provided in this selection, have students identify what characteristics contributed to Dantès' ability.

The above considerations and the read-aloud excerpts could inspire such questions as: How does one learn a second language? Is it easier to learn a third or fourth language than a first or second language? Does age matter? Does motivation matter? What are the best ways to learn another language? Why was Dantès so successful? Can the students imagine having a similar motivation to learn a language? Why are they in this classroom learning a second language? Of what use will this language be to them?

Connecting Second Language Acquisition and Language Arts

After discussing the questions, have students list several components of language. Which of these were helpful to Dantès and how? Which would be helpful to students and how? From this list, several types of writing could follow: a journal entry with reasons for learning a second language, and a letter to Dantès commending him for his clever use of language or asking him specific questions about his process of learning. Have students identify a colloquialism in the second language and describe how its use conveys a command of that language, such as Dantès does while posing as Lord Wilmore. "Heighho" is an antiquated colloquialism; have students generate more modern expressions in English as well as in their second language.

The length of this novel (1,095 pages) may be intimidating to many adolescents. Dumas, like Dickens and Hugo, was paid by the word, so he tended to be verbose. This fact might be interesting to students. Should an author write long books as a commercial venture? Could parts of this novel be condensed without sacrificing literary quality?

This novel has it all: an intricate and adventure-filled plot, with romance, danger, tragedy, and comedy; many well-developed characters; a vivid portrayal of a historical period; excellent depiction of human nature—greed, evil, kindness, love, and irony. For these reasons, *The Count of Monte Cristo* often is required reading in high school English classes, as it was for the characters in the movie *Sleepers*.

Selection 2: A Read-Aloud for Students of English as a Second Language

For this selection, I suggest reading aloud an entire novel, one that is particularly well suited for English as a second language (ESL) learners. For North American students the novel provides insights about ESL learners. As Cook and Gonzales (1995) point out, teaching ESL with literature can illustrate for learners the human experiences that are common to all cultures.

Grab Hands and Run by Frances Temple (1993) is based on stories the author heard when she hosted a Salvadoran family applying for Canadian citizenship. The story is about Felipe and his family, as they live with and then flee from political chaos in El Salvador. The frightening situation is set when Felipe's dog finds a dismembered human hand—a remnant of the army's cruelty. Soon Jacinto, the father, disappears, and Felipe and his family must flee to Canada as their father had told them to do should he ever "disappear." The remainder of the novel details their adventures on their journey to Canada.

We follow Felipe and his family as they covertly cross difficult borders on their way to freedom. They find themselves becoming like chameleons as they work to "fit in" wherever they are, to avoid suspicion. In the United States, they are betrayed and taken to jail. The family is recommended for Canadian citizenship. Free at last, Felipe, Romy, and Paloma can live in Canada.

Specific Excerpts to Address ESL Issues

The 20 chapters of *Grab Hands and Run* are conducive to an interactive reading format. Begin by reading the first two chapters aloud, then alternate students' silent reading with read-alouds throughout the remainder of the book. Because the novel is rich with ESL issues, discussions should occur, at least once during each chapter.

Several brief passages are identified and presented in relation to ESL issues, along with possible questions or comments designed to generate discussion. Have each ESL learner read his or her own copy of this novel, following along as the novel is read aloud to see how the written English words sound in an expressive context. Discussion should encourage not only involvement and critical thinking, but also should provide the much-needed opportunity for and practice in using the English language.

The importance of literacy as the connection between politics, language, and power is built into the story. In North America, learners might take the power of literacy for granted, but many second language learners (L2) do not. Jacinto, for instance, is a highly literate architect who has taught Paloma to read and is sending Felipe and Romy to school. Most children in the El Salvador of this story do not attend school or learn to read. Literacy is viewed with skepticism. The grandfather's and grandmother's remarks make this clear:

> That and his job of drawing pictures to build houses...Ana, how can holding meetings and drawing pictures be work? Truly. How can a man who doesn't sweat find favor with God? (p. 5)
>
> "Look what he writes, Chuy!" says Abuela, showing him the paper. "Felipe's schooling is good." ...With such schooling they'll never take this boy for the army," she says.
>
> "True, they seem to want only illiterates for the army," says my grandfather. (p. 6)

Jacinto is active in the resistance movement. His literacy gives him the power to help make changes in his country; the army prefers illiterates, who will be far less insurgent.

After reading aloud these short selections, ask learners how literacy is regarded in their home countries: Do all children attend school? Is school valued? Is everyone offered the opportunity to learn to read?

In contrast, though Abuela is proud of Felipe's writing, oral tradition is a potent force in this culture. The older women do not write, but they are guardians of oral tradition. They sing and tell stories to the children. Paloma tells stories of Cipitio the Monster to entertain Felipe and Romy; she tells stories of her relationship with Jacinto to inspire; and she tells stories to protect them from trouble as they travel. Felipe and Romy use these stories and others they create to make their hardships on the journey bearable. Ask students in the ESL classroom who remembers stories being told rather than read: When is reading more useful than oral traditions? Less useful? Can both be important?

Another issue for ESL learners is the many challenges to be met as they adapt to North America. As Felipe and his family move from the countryside to the city and from country to country they encounter a variety of cultural situations to which they must adapt. For instance, the same language is spoken with different dialects. In order to adapt, one must know how to express oneself within the circumstances. As Felipe, Romy, and Paloma walk toward freedom, they are warned.

One question about this read-aloud might be, Have you ever noticed that people use different words to express the same meaning? Can you think of examples? For instance, in the United States, midwesterners often say "sack," and northerners say "bag," and some southerners "cut off" lights, while many northerners "turn off" lights.

The excerpt (page 72) also illustrates the issue of acculturation versus assimilation for an L2 or ESL learner. Learners should not think that they have to abandon their own cultures when they learn English. If they feel that they must keep quiet (or be chameleons), they may resent using English. The following questions might help an ESL learner express emotions about this issue: Have you

Read-Aloud From *Grab Hands and Run*

"Walk east," Josefina urges us. "Find a boat. Don't talk any more than you have to. And when you do, remember, we Guatemalans say aldea for village, not cantón."

Josefina has been correcting our Salvadoran way of speaking. "It is not that our Guatemalan way is better, Felipe," she says carefully. "Your way of speaking is beautiful, too. But you don't want to draw attention to yourselves. You need to adapt, to belong everywhere. Like fish in a stream, you need to be."

"Chameleons," says Romy.

"Chameleons with language," says Josefina, smiling. (p. 65)

[From *Grab Hands and Run* by Frances Temple. Copyright ©1993. Reprinted with permission of Orchard Books.]

ever felt safer not saying anything so you would not draw attention to yourself? When did this happen? Do you think that keeping quiet is always the best solution? Is it for Felipe's family?

Following this discussion, read aloud the selection in which Felipe and Romy start attending a school at the detention center.

Ask ESL learners to share their favorite holidays in their homelands. Most likely, the classroom will include learners from several countries, so the exchange will be rich and varied. ESL learners will be practicing listening and speaking about a topic with which they are familiar and interested.

By the time this novel ends, Romy has learned slang. She speaks on the telephone to friends:

"Hi!"
"What's up?"

There are many long pauses. Giggles. The rest of us laugh at her, and Romy makes faces at us. Paloma is of two minds about our having American friends. She wants us to be happy about going to Canada. (p. 163)

Romy has begun to adapt, yet her mother is hesitant, worried that her children may forget their own language and culture. This is an issue of concern for many ESL parents. By reading this selection aloud, conversation can be stimulated about such concerns.

The passage also illustrates how quickly younger children seem to learn a new language. The whole family needed time to become acquainted with North America, but Romy, who is the youngest, is the fastest language learner. Ask students what family member has learned English the fastest, and why.

Read-Aloud From *Grab Hands and Run*

I hate the school. It's late October now, and there is talk of Halloween. This is what the Day of the Dead is called in the United States. Children go in to the streets in costume, my teacher says, and scare people and get candy.

I prefer the way we celebrate the Day of the Dead in El Salvador. Most families have many dead. Everyone who is left in the family gets together a picnic and some candles, and we go to the graveyard. We light the candles and play. The grown-ups tell stories that the people who are dead would have liked, or they sing songs. Then we have the picnic. That is what I would want to do for Jacinto, if he were dead. Eat chili peppers, which he loves. Play hopscotch on his grave. (p. 141)

[From *Grab Hands and Run* by Frances Temple. Copyright ©1993. Reprinted with permission of Orchard Books.]

To learn a second language, informal "lessons" are often the best.

We say thank you many times. We try hard to answer questions in English. We discover jigsaw puzzles, which allow you to lie on the floor quietly playing, listening to the grown-ups—piecing together the conversations, the attitudes of our hosts. (p. 159)

Yet, in schools, ESL learners sometimes study grammar in a formal manner:

We are studying for school, copying verbs in English and muttering them aloud.
"I go
You go
He/she/it goes"
"We go!" yells Paloma triumphantly. "Warden! Warden, please! We go to Canada!" (p. 151)

What is the place of formal grammar lessons, and when is practical usage preferred in ESL classrooms? Leki (1993) cautions that formal language study, specifically rules, should be limited to contexts in which the learner understands and needs to know the rules.

From studies of contrastive grammar (Leki, 1993), we realize that Spanish is often embellished and picturesque when compared to a more direct American style. Certainly, the selections we have given here illustrate the beauty of the Spanish language: Even in the English translation, its poetic, lyrical nature is evident in many of the novel's descriptions, translations, and phrases, as when Felipe describes the uncertainty about his father's safety as "a crater in the middle of our souls" (p. 136). Because all languages vary in style, such a remark made to ESL learners from various backgrounds might encourage a discussion of these differences and lead to a greater appreciation of language.

Lessons From an ESL Tutor

A colleague tutored a 19-year-old Cuban refugee, Frank, using *Grab Hands and Run* extensively with good results. Because Frank was a refugee, as was Felipe, the political aspect of the story caught his interest right away. Without any prompting, Frank read, made margin notes, and looked up vocabulary. Although Frank is an intermediate learner with a wide vocabulary, he found this novel to be a worthwhile challenge. His tutor discovered that Frank could respond to the story and tell additional details. Because listening comprehension was an area in which Frank needed lots of practice, his tutor read chapters to him a few paragraphs at a time and followed with discussion.

Frank's tutor said he learned also from *Grab Hands and Run*. Woven into the story are cultural cues that enlightened him about the richness of Salvadoran customs. The plight of political refugees and the problems many ESL learners face as they learn English became more personalized for him in this novel than in a traditional graduate course. ESL teachers—and all teachers—can learn much about their students' world by reading literature that describes that world.

A Final Point

While true for all learners, working with relevant materials is especially important for ESL learners, who have little background experience with the materials they will study in North American schools. *Grab Hands and Run* is relevant to ESL learners because it addresses important issues L2 learners face.

The dilemmas Felipe, Romy, and Paloma face as they struggle with a new language and culture are universal. Their observations and solutions offer insights for all ESL learners. Using the read-aloud approach is especially suitable, because the ESL learner benefits from listening to the English language while reading along. The read-alouds highlight important issues that can generate discussion. The discussion provides practice in language use as well as understanding about ESL issues, and discussion often is the stimulus for writing.

Brief Selections

A Reluctant Learner

Mei Mei in Levine's (1989) *I Hate English!* does *not* want to learn English. She likes living in Chinatown, where her culture and language surround her. She sees no reason to change. Yet, her teacher patiently expects her to learn English. She resists, but becomes enticed by stories written in English. On a walk with her teacher, she discovers that English might be useful outside of Chinatown.

Mei Mei illustrates the fear a learner can experience, wondering if the native language and culture will be lost. She is fighting to keep what is important to her. She worries that she will forget the words to express herself in Chinese if she uses English too often: "She felt she might lose something" (p. 18). She dreams that she has gone to China and cannot even remember her name

Sometimes a second language learner becomes overloaded with new information. Too much is happening at once and too many new concepts are being introduced. The learner, who seems to be learning quickly, may suddenly regress or stop learning. Mei Mei tells her teacher to "Stop! Forever talking!" (p. 26). Mei Mei cannot take it all in and wants a chance to stop hearing the English all around her. If a learner does not feel comfortable to step back and take it one step at a time, language shock may occur. Time to absorb the overload of information is needed. Mei Mei's teacher does give her plenty of time, knowing that Mei Mei will find her own balance. By the end of this children's novel, Mei Mei herself is forever speaking English, but also recognizes that certain of her thoughts will always be best expressed in Chinese. At the end of the story, Mei Mei " talks in Chinese and English whenever she wants" (p. 30).

I Hate English! is children's literature, so the entire book can be read aloud in a few minutes. Because Levine (1989) ex-presses so well the anguish of a second language learner who feels caught between two worlds, and because of its brevity, this selection has been well-received by secondary students.

Translation Challenges

In the book, *Nineteen Ways of Looking at Wang Wei* (Weinberger & Paz, 1987), two poets offer several translations of Wang Wei's 1,200-year-old poem about deer. French, Spanish, and several English versions are included. For each translation, the poets discuss why the translation works or loses some of the poet's depth. In one of the authors' favorite translations, by Gary Snyder, they note how he changes tense to bring the poem fully to an English speaker:

> Changing the passive *is heard* to the imperative *hear* is particularly beautiful, and not incorrect; it creates an exact moment, which is now. Giving us both meanings, *sounds and echoes*, for the last word of line 2 is, like most sensible ideas, revolutionary. Translators always assume that only one reading of a foreign word or phrase may be presented, despite the fact that perfect correspondence is rare. (p. 43)

Students should find listening to each version of the poem interesting. Have them decide which version they prefer before the views of Weinberger and Paz are presented. Poetry cries to be read aloud. This book offers an excellent opportunity not only for the read-aloud, but also for discovering the intricacies of different languages and the challenges of translating them.

Conclusion

The point of this chapter is not to argue the pros and cons of required versus self-selected reading in a school setting. I am not advocating that foreign language teachers require their students to read *The Count of Monte Cristo.* The point is to demonstrate how a person may come to read a certain book because of some influence, often unexpected and serendipitous. I had never considered reading *The Count of Monte Cristo* until I saw the movie *Sleepers,* but I figured that if the novel could be so influential to these young characters, it must have something to offer me. And, because I am currently studying language acquisition, the passages in the excerpt jumped out at me. An ulterior motive for introducing this read-aloud is to introduce to otherwise skeptical adolescents a novel that many would enjoy, especially if it is not required. At least, they might "tuck away" the idea and read *The Count of Monte Cristo* later.

Thinking about language may be new to many adolescents. *Nineteen Ways of Looking at Wang Wei* might break the ice and also supplement a lesson on poetry. Many adolescents would be drawn to *Grab Hands and Run* for the adventure in the story. But, they will also learn a great deal about the adversity many people face daily, especially the language barriers people face when traveling through different countries. *I Hate English!* illustrates this same lesson in an appealing manner.

Read-Alouds for Special Populations

8

Learning to read is especially difficult for older learners or those with learning disabilities. In this chapter, selections are presented for each of these groups. However, the content and instructional suggestions for each excerpt can also be used in content areas. The selections are varied in genre including an essay, a young adult novel, a mystery, and a "real-life" clip from Paul Harvey.

Selection 1: Of Libraries and Adult Beginning Readers

An essay from Barbara Kingsolver's (1995) *High Tide in Tucson* is the inspiration for this read-aloud. The intended audience is adult beginning readers, although the excerpt could be read to secondary students also. The story is true, amusing, and inspiring. The author is a writer of fiction, nonfiction, and poetry, and is best known for her novel, *Pigs in Heaven*, a *New York Times* bestseller. Most of the writing is based, loosely, on her own life. She shares her memories from her childhood in southern Appalachia and the experiences of her adult life in southern Arizona. Before becoming a writer, the author trained as a biologist, which may explain why her writings are rich with detail of the natural world.

The 17 essays in *High Tide in Tucson*, are interrelated and intended to be read in sequence; however, each essay easily stands on its own. The excerpt on page 79 comes from the essay "How Mr. Dewey Decimal Saved My Life." The essay was originally part of an address given to the American Library Association Convention in 1993. Kingsolver describes her experiences in a rural high school in Kentucky. Back in the 1960s, she explains, a school's funding depended on the wealth of the county where it was located. This meant that in depressed areas, like her county, there was not much money to bring enrichment programs to the public schools. Her adventure in the school library is the beginning of a new world for her. The essay begins by claiming that a librarian named Miss Truman Richey saved her life. As the story unfolds, the author demonstrates her talent for capturing her feelings and attitudes as a teenager struggling to make meaning out of the awkward years of high school.

If time is at a premium, this short read-aloud passage would be enough to stimulate any number of instructional activities. If time is not restricted, then the entire 8-page essay could be read aloud.

Why This Read-Aloud for Adult Beginning Readers?

The author relates her own struggles in becoming educated. Because she is writing for other adults, her story might help put adult beginning readers at ease. Reminiscing is sometimes a positive way to encourage discussion and introspection. Kingsolver's tone respects the adult reader—or listener. Her message can be encouraging to an adult beginning reader who faces huge hurdles in becoming literate.

Some adult beginning readers are reluctant to visit a library. Being near so many books and readers in an environment where they do not excel can create discomfort—or even provoke negative associations. Other adult beginning readers may simply feel that the library is not a place where they would—or should—visit. Yet, the library can be a wonderful place for quiet study and lessons, with rich resource material all around. Also, many volunteer organizations encourage the use of the library as an excellent location for tutoring sessions. Overcoming any negative associations with the library could be one result of using this read-aloud while teaching an adult beginning reader.

Adult beginning readers will become more assured as readers when they can begin to ask and answer questions by using books as a major resource. Personal inquiry is a wonderful way to stimulate reading at any level. What better place to begin an inquiry than in the library?

Specific Activities for Adult Beginning Readers

The excerpt could precede an initial visit to the library. Kingsolver tells a personal story about how the library became so important to her. What is the adult learner's perception of the library? Has he

Read-Aloud From *High Tide in Tucson*

Miss Richey had something else in mind. She took me by the arm in study hall one day and said, "Barbara, I'm going to teach you Dewey Decimal."

One more valuable skill in my life.

She launched me on the project of cataloging and shelving every one of the, probably, thousand books in the Nicholas County High School library. And since it beat Home Ec III by a mile, I spent my study-hall hours this way without audible complaint, so long as I could look plenty surly while I did it. Though it was hard to see the real point of organizing books nobody ever looked at. And since it was my God-given duty in those days to be frank as a plank, I said as much to Miss Richey.

She just smiled. She with her hidden agenda. And gradually, in the process of handling every book in the room, I made some discoveries. I found "Gone With the Wind," which I suspected my mother felt was kind of trashy, and I found Edgar Allan Poe, who scared me witless. I found that the call number for books about snakes is 666. I found William Saroyan's "Human Comedy," down there on the shelf between Human Anatomy and Human Physiology, where probably no one had touched it since 1943. But I read it, and it spoke to me. In spite of myself I imagined the life of an immigrant son who believed human kindness was a tangible and glorious thing. I began to think about words like tangible and glorious. I read on. After I'd read all the good ones, I went back and read Human Anatomy and Human Physiology and found that I liked those pretty well too. (pp. 48–49)

[From *High Tide in Tucson* by Barbara Kingsolver Copyright ©1995. New York: HarperCollins.]

or she had a pleasant or negative experience? How comfortable is the learner with the idea of visiting a library? Discussion can alleviate possible concerns.

For the first activity, prepare the learner to find specific books in the library. Depending on the library and the learner, this may require explanation and instruction on the recent computerization of some library catalogs. Learning how to use a card catalog or database can be intimidating, but can be mastered by following a sequence of steps that can be taught. By dramatizing or role-playing, the adult can practice locating resources and become more confident and familiar with procedures before visiting the library.

Develop a list of learner interests, which could serve as a starting point for finding the new reader a book that would spark interest. For such a lesson, explain what the Dewey Decimal System is and how useful it has been over many years to classify and locate books. What is the Dewey Decimal System? What is the point of organizing books? Where would the topics human anatomy or human physiology be found using the Dewey Decimal System? Knowing about Mr. Dewey Decimal could demystify the library for many otherwise intimidated adult new readers.

What was the high school like where the adult beginning reader attended? Was it as poor as Kingsolver's? Would its ranking in spending have been lower than 51st, as Kingsolver claims for her school? Were girls expected to take home ec and boys to take shop? What resources were available to keep teenagers busy? Kingsolver remarks that "nothing was required of me at Nicholas County High that was going to keep me off the streets." An adult beginning reader may look back and remember high school as "a state of unrest."

Although discussion about one's own school environment is a kind of personal history lesson, a more general discussion of events in the 1960s when Kingsolver was in high school in Kentucky would provide the stimulus for a good history lesson. Most adult beginning readers today would have some personal knowledge of the 1960s, which could be placed in the perspective of national and international events of the time.

Language Arts Activities for Adult Beginning Readers

This essay is rich with possibilities for instruction in the language arts. Kingsolver starts the essay,

> Salvation is such a heady thing the temptation is to dance gasping on the shore, shouting that we are alive, till our forgotten savior has long since gone under. (p. 46)

What does this sentence mean? How can it be paraphrased, and would a paraphrase capture the meaning and the reader as effectively? We often fail to thank those people in our lives who have helped us the most. Have the adult learner think of a person who has been a major source of help in his or her life and explain who that person is and what that person did. Next, have them compose a thank-you letter, that can be shared orally and, if appropriate, mailed to that person.

The read-aloud could also serve as a springboard for a creative writing activity about something or someone the learner remembers as special from childhood. Kingsolver uses personal experience as a basis for her writing. The adult beginning reader could use personal experience to create an essay or to dictate a story for a language experience activity.

There are many opportunities for vocabulary development in this essay. Because Kingsolver writes of her fun in finding new words in books and making them "her own," encourage learners to identify unknown words from this excerpt that could be added to their vocabularies. For instance, she mentions *tangible* and *glorious*. What do these words mean? How do they describe human kindness?

What is Miss Richey's "hidden agenda?" Was Miss Richey successful? Has the adult learner ever heard of Mitchell's *Gone With the Wind*, Poe, or Saroyan? Discussions about and excerpts from these authors might be shared if interest is generated. Is there an author the adult learner has always wondered about?

Another wonderful story about the library is found in *Rufus M* (1943) by Eleanor Estes. In the first chapter of this novel, Rufus learns to write his name so that he can get a library card. He has to go to great lengths to do so and becomes well acquainted with the librarian in the process. If the adult beginning readers appreciate Kingsolver's library experience, they might well enjoy Rufus M.'s adventures. Because this is a novel for children, however, it might work better as a sequel to "How Mr. Dewey Decimal Saved My Life." *Rufus M.* is also a rich resource for a history lesson.

Although this essay and the books by Kingsolver might be too difficult for a new reader to tackle independently, they offer opportunities to share with the learner about writing, which paints vivid pictures of people, places, and events. Reading one work by Kingsolver will make one hungry to read more of her writings. Adult new readers might also want to "travel" with this author, or others, through a series of written journeys. Bon voyage!

Brief Selection

A Late Start in Literacy

Many adults mask quite masterfully their inability to read well. Yet if they discover a sympathetic mentor, they are relieved to admit their struggle and hopeful about learning to read. There are many reasons why some individuals reach adulthood without learning to read well. Sometimes a learning disability is the cause, compounded by lack of a strong educational support system. Dicey, in the novel *Dicey's Song* (Voigt, 1982), is surprised to discover that her boss, Millie, cannot read well enough to place correct orders for her own grocery store. Millie had ordered corn*flakes* when she had meant to order corn*chips*. They solve the immediate problem of too many boxes of cornflakes by running a special and reordering cornchips. But the major problem is that Millie needs help with the order forms.

Dicey thinks the order form looks pretty simple. She asks, "How can you make mistakes on this?" (p. 42). Millie replies, "Because I never learned to read properly. I can't even read a newspaper. You didn't know that, did you? You didn't know what a stupid old woman you were working for" (p. 43). Millie explains that she had trouble learning in school, and finally quit. Her husband had helped her with the orders and bills in their store until he died. Millie says, "Of course I can read. I just take so long at it, and the words all look alike" (p. 43).

See the activities suggested for the next selection (page 83), which will work well for this excerpt. In addition, use this read-aloud with secondary students to point out that many people cover up their inability to read just as Millie does, however, they do not necessarily feel happy about it like Millie does. Ask if students know anyone who has not learned to read efficiently. How do these people manage in a reading world? What support do they have when they need to use literacy skills? What could be a solution for Millie?

A Read-Aloud for Discussing Disabilities

For avid readers of mystery, Jonathan Kellerman's (1988) *The Butcher's Theater* is for you. Set in Jerusalem, Israel, a detective solves a series of murders committed by a psychopath who surgically removes women's organs and drains their blood. Kellerman presents the killer's own voice through flashback and stream-of-consciousness prose, which describes the killer's warped childhood. The detective is the other voice of humanity and intelligence, carefully following leads and meticulously eliminating suspects. The background setting and information about cultural conflicts between Arabs and Jews are well described. Kellerman draws on his own knowledge as a clinical psychologist to paint the killer's portrait.

Daniel (Dani) Sharavi, the detective, is a Yemenite Jew, descended from a race not entirely accepted in the Jewish community. He is small and physically disabled as a result of a wound suffered in the Israeli War of 1967. His left arm is disfigured and his hand is useless. In spite of his disability, he has risen in the detective ranks and is a well-respected *pakad* (captain). Avi Cohen is a fresh, young detective assigned to this, his first, case. He seems arrogant, rich, and affected. When Dani first sees Avi, he is not impressed.

A man was in the lobby, leaning against the mailboxes, smoking. Young, twenty-two or -three, well built and tan, with dark wavy hair and a full clipped beard highlighted with ginger, wearing a white polo shirt with a Fila logo, American designer jeans, brand-new blue-and-white Nike running shoes. On his left wrist was an expensive-looking watch with a gold band; around his neck, a gold Hai charm. An American, thought Daniel. Some kind of playboy, maybe a rich student. (p. 107)

During the investigation, Avi is assigned to the tedious detail of checking files. This job takes him a great deal longer than it should because he has dyslexia: He describes his struggle as "A flood of words, clogging him, choking him, making his head reel" (p. 138). So, when Dani asks him to write the final draft of a report, Avi refuses, saying that he will quit instead. Dani has predicted this response and then draws Avi into a conversation about overcoming disabilities. Dani compares his disabled arm to Avi's dyslexia and encourages Avi to find a way to overcome his problem.

Activities for Discussing Disabilities

This read-aloud creates an awareness of what disabilities are and how to acknowledge them. A regular or special education teacher could read this excerpt as a way to begin discussion of disabilities. Some are physical, as Dani Sharavi's is, and some are neurological, as Avi Cohen's is. In either case, the disability has greatly affected each person's outlook and job performance, and even the selection of a career. In what ways do disabilities affect performance? Can disabilities be cured?

Students may better understand that a disability is not correctable, but one can learn to compensate. How does Dani Sharavi work around his disability? How does Avi Cohen work around his disability? When he finds he cannot complete a task efficiently, his solution is to quit rather than to com-

pensate. What should Avi Cohen's solution be? Have students suggest solutions. Ask if they know of anyone with similar disabilities and challenges. How do they cope?

Introduce students to different definitions of disability and have them apply these definitions to Dani and Avi. Specifically, a professional definition of *learning disability* could lead to identifying features of dyslexic children Dani Sharavi speaks of in the read-aloud. Using the federal definition of learning disabilities, students can discuss what constitutes a person with disabilities. This will help broaden their awareness of the issues, as well as the personal aspects presented in this read-aloud.

Is learning to read a difficult process, as it seemed when Sharavi observed the children and adults in the read-aloud? Ask students how difficult learning to read was for them. Why would the tasks assigned to Avi be so difficult? Could he have been a good detective without being able to accomplish such tasks?

Activities for Exploring Language Arts

Encourage students to list what they know—or think they know—about disabilities. I call this "factstorming" (Richardson, 1996), like the first step in K-W-L (Ogle, 1986). At this point, have students search for more information to confirm, disprove, or augment what they know by reading newspaper articles, searching the Internet, or reading the Richardson–Pikulski (1997) debate

Read-Aloud From *The Butcher's Theater*

"I can't do it, Pakad."

"Can't do what?"

"Anything. I'm going to quit the police force." Blurted it out, just like that, though he hadn't come to a decision about it yet.

The little Yemenite had nodded as if he'd expected it. Stared at him with those gold-colored eyes and said, "Because of the dyslexia?"

It had been his turn to stare then, nodding dumbly, in shock, as Sharavi kept talking.

"Mefakeah Shmeltzer told me you take an extraordinary amount of time to read things. Lose your place a lot and have to start all over again. I called your high school and they told me about it."

"I'm sorry," Avi had said, feeling stupid the moment the words left his lips. He'd trained himself long a go not to apologize.

"Why?" asked Sharavi. "Because you have an imperfection?"

"I'm just not suited for police work."

Sharavi held up his left hand, showed him the scars, a real mess.

"I can't box with bad guys, Cohen, so I concentrate on using my brains."

"That's different."

Sharavi shrugged. "I'm not going to try to talk you into it. It's your life. But you might think of giving yourself some more time. Now that I know about you, I could keep you away from paperwork. Concentrate on your strengths." Smiling: "If you have any." (p. 174)

The Yemenite had taken him for a cup of coffee, asked him about his problem, gotten him to talk more than anyone ever had. A master interrogator, he realized later. Made you feel good about opening up.

"I know a little bit about dyslexia," he had said, looking down at his bad hand. "After '67, I spent two months in a rehabilitation center—Beit Levinsteing, near Ra'nana—working on getting some function back in the hand. There were kids there with learning problems, a few adults too. I watched them struggle, learning special ways to read. It seemed like a very difficult process." (p. 174) in *Reading Today*. From their findings, have students review their initial list and revise it, reformulating their knowledge, as in a PreP activity (Langer, 1981). Ask them to look for portrayals of individuals with disabilities in the literature they read and discuss them in class. For instance, in *Dicey's Song* (1982), Millie reveals to Dicey that she mixes up orders for her store because, although she can read, "I just take so long at it, and the words all look alike" (p. 43).

Have students write either a journal entry of their reactions to the read-aloud or a response to probing questions about its effect. Have students write about a personal experience or event that helped them to better understand people with disabilities.

Although there are specific laws defining the accommodations for physically disabled, these accommodations are often not satisfactory or available. Have students research available accommodations in their community and write a report of their findings:

A Brief Selection About Winning From Failure

In his radio program, Paul Harvey delivered inspiring stories of real people who made success from failure. His son-in-law, Paul Aurandt, collected several of these stories in *Destiny* (1983). These stories can be read aloud to high school students when they feel defeated by academics or life events. They have fun guessing who the hero of the story actually is.

In "Sparky Was a Loser," Harvey recounts a child's constant failures in school, academically and athletically. He was socially awkward as well. However, he loved to draw. Walt Disney's studio did not think much of his submissions to them but, he persevered and became a famous cartoonist. He is, of course, Charles Monroe Schultz, who created "Peanuts," a comic strip that depicts Charlie Brown, another loser.

> Sparky was a loser. He, his classmates, everyone knew it. So he rolled with it. Sparky made up his mind early in life that if things were meant to work out, they would. Otherwise, he would content himself with what appeared to be inevitable mediocrity. (p. 85)

[From *Destiny* by Paul Aurandt (1983). Bantam Books/ William Morrow Publishing Company.]

Ask students to predict who Sparky is after reading aloud this excerpt. If the entire account is read, pause for predictions at intervals. Discuss vocabulary, for instance, *mediocrity*. Why is this such an appropriate word in the context of the story? Ask students if they know anyone from history who seemed to be "a loser" and whether this person ultimately succeeded. Ask them to think about anyone they know who is unsuccessful. What might they predict for this unsuccessful person in the future? Assign an essay in which they write " the rest of the story" about one of these situations. Students have a lot of fun with this read-aloud and almost always feel perked up as they leave class.

Conclusion

In Chapter 1, a principle for selecting and using read-alouds is that the selection should "tie reading to pleasure, not pain" (Chandler, 1997). Kingsolver and Kellerman both convey to readers how painful it can be to be different, yet they do so in ways that both entertain and educate readers at the same time. What could be more inspiring and pleasurable than to realize that out of a painful childhood full of failure came a popular comic strip? That is why these excerpts are successful read-alouds.

Afterword

The selections in this book are intended to be representative, not exhaustive. You will see from these selections that many possibilities exist for using literature read-alouds in content classrooms. You are encouraged to modify, mix and match, and create. You may like a selection but prefer to use different activities. Or, you may like an activity but would like to use it with other selections.

The number of possibilities is as great as the number of books available to us. Appendix B lists more selections, with just a sentence about each. I am grateful for the recommendations of my students in compiling this list. I wish I had the time and space to share more from my own collection, but I know you will assemble a collection more suitable for your own needs.

Begin to look at literature in new ways. Authors give so much to readers. Not only do they share with us the elements of plot and content, style, voice, setting, characters, and theme and thesis, they also teach as they entertain. Reading literature is truly an education. Share this with your students.

Perhaps you remember the story in *The Phantom Tollbooth* of the Dodecahedron explaining to Milo that a beaver 68 feet long with a 51-foot tail could build Boulder Dam? When Milo points out the absurdity of this, the Dodecahedron replies, "If you want sense, you have to make it yourself" (p. 175). Read alouds make the best sense when *you* discover them and their many uses.

Appendix A

List of Read-Alouds Introduced in This Book

Aardema, V. (1992). *Why mosquitoes buzz in people's ears: A West African tale.* New York: Penguin.

Aurandt, P. (1983). *Destiny.* New York: Bantam, William Morrow.

Burns, M. (1975). *The I hate mathematics! book.* New York: Little, Brown.

Cary, J. (1952). *Mr. Johnson.* London: Michael Joseph.

Chappell, F. (1991). *More shapes than one.* New York: St. Martin's.

Choi, S.N.(1991). *The year of impossible goodbyes.* New York: Houghton Mifflin.

Cushman, K. (1994). *Catherine, called Birdy.* New York: Houghton Mifflin.

Dillard, A. (1974). *Pilgrim at Tinker Creek.* New York: HarperCollins.

Dillard, A. (1990). *An American childhood.* New York: HarperCollins.

Dumas, A. (1852). *The Count of Monte Cristo.* London: Oxford University Press.

Edgerton, C. (1985). *Raney.* Chapel Hill, NC: Algonquin Books; New York: Workman.

Estes, E. (1943). *Rufus M.* New York: Harcourt Brace, Jovanovich.

Flaubert, G. (1902). *Madame Bovary.* New York: Collier.

Frazier, C. (1997). *Cold Mountain.* New York: Atlantic Monthly Press.

Hamilton, V. (1995). *Many thousand gone: African Americans from slavery to freedom.* New York: Knopf.

Harris, E. (1988). *Mississippi solo: A river quest.* New York: Harper & Row.

Juster, N. (1964). *The phantom tollbooth.* New York: Random House.

Keats, J. (1959). *On first looking into Chapman's Homer.* In D. Bush (Ed.), *Selected poems and letters of Keats.* Itasca, IL: Riverside. (First published in 1816)

Kellerman, J. (1988). *The butcher's theater.* New York: Bantam Books, Bantam Doubleday Dell.

Kingsolver, B. (1995) *High tide in Tucson*. New York: HarperCollins.

Lampton, C. (1988). *Endangered species*. New York: Franklin Watts.

Levine, E. (1989). *I hate English!* New York: Scholastic.

Lowry, L. (1979). *Anastasia Krupnik*. New York: Houghton Mifflin.

Merrill, J. (1964). *The pushcart wars*. New York: Harper & Row.

Mullane, M. (1996). *Lift off! An astronaut's dream*. New York: Silver-Burdett.

Musgrove, M. (1976). *Ashanti to Zulu: African traditions*. New York: Dial.

Neville, K. (1988). *The eight*. New York: Ballantine.

Paulsen, G. (1993). *Nightjohn*. New York: Delacorte.

Pratchett, T. (1983). *The colour of magic*. London/Buckinghamshire, UK: Colin Smythe.

Pratchett, T. (1988). *Wyrd sisters*. London: Victor Gollancy.

Pratchett, T. (1991). *Witches abroad*. London: Victor Gollancy.

Price, L. (1990). *Aida* (illustrated by Leo and Diane Dillon). New York: Gulliver, Harcourt Brace.

Rhyne, N. (1997). *The ghost of Hampton Plantation*. Orangeburg, SC: Sandlapper.

Sartre, J.P. (1964). *Words*. New York: George Braziller.

Shelley, M. (1994). *Frankenstein*, Mineola, NY: Dover. (Originally published in 1831)

Simon, H. (1960). *100 great operas and their stories*. New York: Doubleday.

Smith, L. (1988). *Fair and tender ladies*. New York: G.P. Putnam's Sons.

Staples, S.F. (1993). *Haveli*. New York: Knopf.

Temple, F. (1993). *Grab hands and run*. New York: Orchard Books.

Tepper, S. (1987). *After long silence*. New York: Bantam.

Twain, M. (1917). *Life on the Mississippi*. New York: Harper & Row.

Vickers, H. (1979). *Great operatic disasters* New York: St. Martin's Griffin Books.

Voigt, C. (1982). *Dicey's song*. New York: Antheneum.

Voigt, C. (1983). *A solitary blue*. New York: Atheneum.

Walsh, M. (1994). *Who's afraid of opera?* New York: Simon and Schuster.

Weinberger, E., & Paz, O. (1987). *Nineteen ways of looking at Wang Wei*. Wakefield, RI: Moyer Bell.

White, E.B. (1951). *The second tree from the corner*. New York: Harper & Row.

Wodehouse, P.G. (1938) *The code of the Woosters*. New York: Random House.

The Possibilities: Read-Alouds in This Book and Other Recommendations

For Science

Bryson, B. (1998). *A walk in the woods*. New York: Broadway Books.

Bryson describes walking the Appalachian Trail. We receive a sense of our place in the natural world.

Morrell, V. (1999). The variety of life. *National Geographic, 195*(2), 6–41.
    Without the long-tongued fly, a species of plant would be extinct.

Pirsig, R. (1974). *Zen and the art of motorcycle maintenance: An inquiry into values.* New York: William Morrow.
    The author ponders about ancient man: "ghosts and spirits are quite as real as atoms, particles, photons and quants…" (p. 40–41).

Szentgyorgyi, T. (1999). They don't let sleeping dogs lie. *Popular Science, 254*(3), 35.
    Describes how the author takes tissue samples from bears in their dens, and includes a description of muscle tissue.

See also the following authors whose selections are presented in Chapter 2 of this text: Dillard, Frazier, Lampton, and Mullane.

For Mathematics

Juster, N. (1964). *The phantom tollbooth.* New York: Random House.
    The Dodecahedron tells the word problem about a beaver who could build Boulder Dam.

Rhoads, R., Milauskas, G., & Whipple, R. (1991). *Geometry for enjoyment and challenge.* New York: McDougal, Little.
    In "A Letter to Students," the authors explain in relevant, entertaining fashion why one studies geometry and its many uses.

Voigt, C. (1982). *Dicey's song.* New York: Antheneum/Macmillan.
    Dicey teaches Maybeth about fractions (p. 14).

See also the following authors whose selections are presented in Chapter 3: Burns, Cushman, Neville, Pratchett, and Twain.

For Social Studies

Equiano, O. (1997). Narrative of the life of Olaudah Equiano. In N.Y. McKay (Ed.), *The Norton anthology of African-American literature.* New York: Norton. (Original work published in 1789)
    Describes Equiano's native homeland and new life as a slave.

Orwell, G. (1995). Politics and the English language. In W. Smart (Ed.), *Eight modern essayists.* New York: St. Martin's.
    If people will take the time to think and write clearly and carefully, political regeneration will occur.

Wulffson, D. (1981). *Extraordinary stories behind the invention of ordinary things.* New York: Lothrop, Lee & Shepard.

See annotation under "For Reading" on the next page.

See also the following authors whose selections are presented in Chapter 4: Edgerton, Harris, Keats, Merrill, Rhyne, Twain, and Wodehouse.

For English

Haley, A. (1965). *How I discovered words: A homemade education.* New York: Random House.

Haley writes with Malcolm X's help about how Malcolm X educated himself in prison, learning a wide vocabulary and writing skills.

Kirby, D., Liner, T., & Vinz, R. (1998). *Inside out: Developing strategies for teaching writing and style.* Portsmouth, NH: Boynton/Cook.

The essay, "Mad Talking, Soft Talking, Fast Talking" is a good introduction to the nature of writing and the concepts of voice and style.

Wulffson, D. (1981). *Extraordinary stories behind the invention of ordinary things.* New York: Lothrop, Lee & Shepard.

See annotation under "For Reading."

See also the following authors whose selections are presented in Chapter 5: Cary, Chappell, Flaubert, Keats, Lowry, Smith, White, and Wordsworth.

For Music, Art, and Physical Education

The Caldecott Aesop: Twenty fables. (1978). Garden City, NY: Doubleday.

"The Tortoise and the Hare" is a classic fable of perseverance versus native skill. (PE)

Chatwin, B. (1987). *Songlines.* New York: Elizabeth Sifton/Viking.

Chatwin tells of aborigines and how they find their way across the continent of Australia using song as their "map." (Music)

See the following authors whose selections are presented in Chapter 6: Aurandt (PE); Aardema, Musgrove (Art); Price, Tepper, Simon, Vickers, Voigt, Walsh (Music).

For Language Study

Athanassakis, A.N. (1983). *Hesiad, work and days.* Baltimore, MD: Johns Hopkins University Press.

Hesiod's epic poem helps Latin students understand the culture of his time.

Schafer, P. et al. (1973). *Poems, piece, prose*. New York: Oxford University Press.
"Chanson d'automne" (Song of Autumn) by Paul Verlaine is a wonderful example for French students of sounds, rhythm, tone, and emotive qualities.
See the following authors whose selections are presented in Chapter 7: Choi, Dumas, Levine, Temple, and Weinberger.

For Special Populations

Morrison, T. (1977). *Song of Solomon*. New York: Knopf.
Because he cannot read, Macon Dead "receives" his name from a drunk registrar (p. 53). (Adult beginning reader)
Paulsen, G. (1993). *Nightjohn*. New York: Delacorte Press.
Nightjohn is a former slave who risks his life returning to the South to teach slaves reading and writing. (Adult beginning reader and learning disabilities)
Tan, A. (1991). *The kitchen god's wife*. New York: Random House.
Throughout the novel are selections about how the protagonist taught others to read and write. (Adult beginning reader and learning disabilities)
See the following authors whose selections are presented in Chapter 8: Aurandt, Kingsolver, and Kellerman.

For Reading

Wulffson, D. (1981). *Extraordinary stories behind the invention of ordinary things*. New York: Lothrop, Lee & Shepard Books.
This series of short, true stories tells as much about the people as their inventions, so excerpts could be used in every content area. You will find the book in the children's section of the library. My favorites are the stories about the invention of the alphabet, and books.
See the following authors whose selections are presented in this text: Estes (Chapter 8); Kingsolver (Chapter 8); Pratchett (Chapters 3 and 5); and Sartre (Chapter 1).

Appendix B

Columns Originally Published in the *Journal of Adolescent & Adult Literacy*

A read-aloud for science classrooms, 38(1), September 1994.

A read-aloud for science, 39(6), March 1996. Judy S. Richardson & Margaret Breen.

A read-aloud for science in space, 40(4), January 1997. Judy S. Richardson & Nancy S. Smith.

A read-aloud for mathematics classrooms, 38(3), November 1994.

A read-aloud for algebra and geography classes, 39(4), December–January 1996. Judy S. Richardson & Mark A. Forget.

A read-aloud for math, 40(6), March 1997. Judy S. Richardson & Ena Gross.

A read-aloud for social studies classrooms, 38(5), February 1995.

A read-aloud for cultural diversity, 39(2), October 1995.

A read-aloud for English classrooms, 39(8), May 1996. Judy S. Richardson & R. Jeffrey Cantrell.

A read-aloud for romantics and realists, 40(8), May 1997. Judy S. Richardson, Dennis B. Wimer, & Julie Counts.

An operatic read-aloud for music and art, 41(6), March 1998. Jane Brady Matanzo & Judy S. Richardson.

A read-aloud for music classrooms, 38(7), April 1995.

A read-aloud for foreign languages: Becoming a language master, 41(4), December–January 1998.

A read-aloud for students of English as a second language, 40(2), October 1996. Judy S. Richardson & Lee Carlton.

A read-aloud for adult beginning readers, 41(2), October 1997. Judy S. Richardson & Mary Seward.

A read-aloud for discussing disabilities, 41(8), May 1998. Judy S. Richardson & Joseph Boyle.

Other Sources

Richardson, J.S. (1997). Those wonderful toys: Read-alouds from the classics and assorted literature. In *Exploring Literacy*, W.M. Linek, & E.G. Sturtevant, (Eds.), Yearbook of the College Reading Association.

References

Artley, A.S. (1975). Good teachers of reading—who are they? *The Reading Teacher, 29,* 26–31.

Baumann, J.F., & Duffy, A.M. (1997). *Engaged reading for pleasure and learning: A report for the National Reading Research Center.* Athens, GA: National Reading Research Center

Bintz, W.P. (1993). Resistant readers in secondary education: Some insights and implications. *Journal of Reading, 36,* 604–614.

Bintz, W.P. (1997). Exploring reading nightmares of middle and secondary teachers. *Journal of Adolescent & Adult Literacy, 41,* 2–24.

Cassidy, J. (1984). The devil's dictionary. *Reading Today, 1*(4), 149.

Chandler, K. (1997). The Beach Book Club: Literacy in the "lazy days of summer." *Journal of Adolescent & Adult Literacy, 41,* 104–115.

Cook, L., & Gonzales, P. (1995). Zones of contact: Using literature with second language users. *Reading Today, 12,* p. 27.

Daisy, P. (1993). Three ways to promote the values and uses of literacy at any age. *Journal of Reading, 36,* 436–440.

Duchein, M., & Mealey, D. (1993). Remembrance of books past...long past—Glimpses into aliteracy. *Reading Research and Instruction, 33,* 13–28.

Elley, W.D. (1992). *How in the world do students read? IEA Study of Reading Literacy.* The Hague, The Netherlands: International Association for the Evaluation of Educational Achievement.

Gallagher, J.M (1987). Commentary: Read with your eyes; listen with your heart. *Journal of Reading, 31,* 4–8.

Langer, J. (1981). From theory to practice: A prereading plan. *Journal of Reading, 25,* 152–156.

Leki, L. (1992). *Understanding ESL writers: A guide for teachers.* Portsmouth, NH: Boyton/Cook.

Levinson, B. (Director). (1996). *Sleepers* [Film]. Los Angeles: Warner Bros.

Martin, P. (1993). Capture silk: Reading aloud together. *English Journal, 82,* 16–24.

Megyeri, K.A. (1993). The reading aloud of ninth-grade writing. *Journal of Reading, 37,* 184–190.

National Council of Teachers of Mathematics. (1989). *Curriculum and evaluation standards for school mathematics.* Reston, VA: Author.

National Council of Teachers of Mathematics. (1991). *Professional standards for teaching mathematics.* Reston, VA: Author.

Nilsen, A.P., & Donelson, K. (1997). *Literature for today's young adults.* New York: Longman.

Norton, D. (1992). *The impact of literature-based reading.* New York: Macmillan.

Ogle, D. (1986). K-W-L: A teaching model that develops active reading of expository text. *The Reading Teacher, 39,* 564–570.

Ralph, J., & Crouse, J. (1997). *Reading and mathematics achievement: Growth in high school* (Issue brief) Washington, DC: U.S. Department of Education, Office of Educational Research and Improvement.

Richardson, J. (1981). Mind grabbers, or read aloud to college students too! *ADsig Journal, 3,* 39–51.

Richardson, J. (1994). Coordinating teacher read-alouds with content instruction in secondary classrooms. In G. Cramer & M. Castle (Eds.), *Fostering the love of reading: The affective domain in reading education.* Newark, DE: International Reading Association.

Richardson, J.S. (1996). *An English teacher's survival guide: Reaching and teaching adolescents.* Scarborough and Toronto, ON: Pippin

Richardson, J., & Morgan, R. (1997). *Reading to learn in the content areas, Supporting the textbook with literature.* Belmont, CA: Wadsworth.

Richardson, S., & Pikulski, J. (1997, June/July). Letters to the editor. *Reading Today, 14,* 31.

Routman, R. (1991). *Invitations.* Portsmouth, NH: Heinemann.

Smith, M. (1993). *Kids' book of magic tricks.* Wilton, CT: Watermill Press.

Trelease, J. (1989). *The new read-aloud handbook.* New York: Viking Press.

Trelease, J. (1992). *Hey! Listen to this: Stories to read aloud.* New York: Viking Press.

Index

Page references in *italics* indicate figures.

I–K

L

Y–Z